# Living with Wisdom

## A Life of Thomas Merton

John Howard Griffin

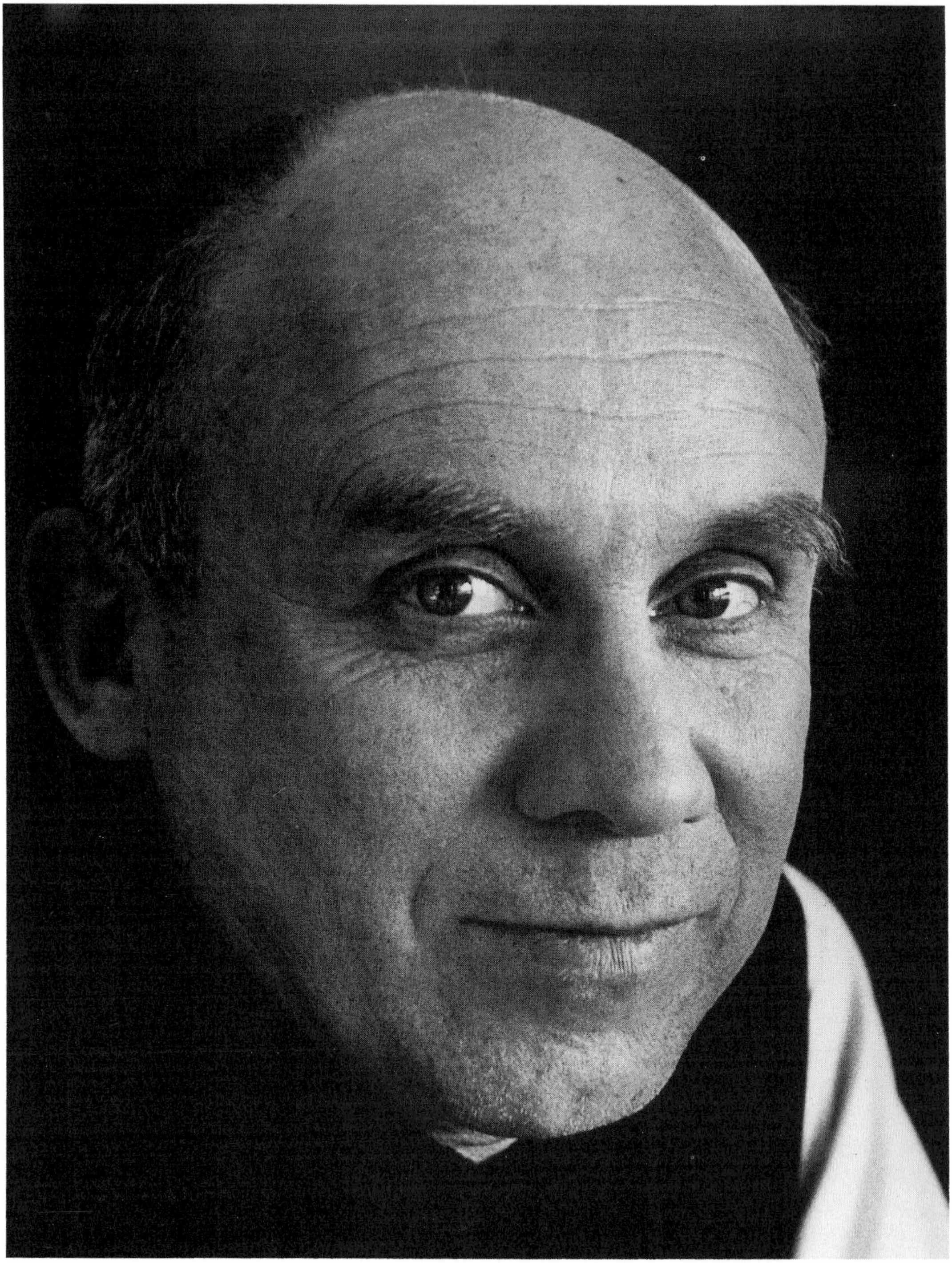

# Living with Wisdom

## A Life of Thomas Merton

Jim Forest

ORBIS BOOKS

Maryknoll, New York 10545

The Catholic Foreign Mission Society of America (Maryknoll) recruits and trains people for overseas missionary service. Through Orbis Books, Maryknoll aims to foster the international dialogue that is essential to mission. The books published, however, reflect the opinions of their authors and are not meant to represent the official position of the society.

Copyright © 1991 by James H. Forest
Published by Orbis Books, Maryknoll, NY 10545
All rights reserved
Manufactured in the United States of America

Second Printing, February 1992

Acknowledgments
Excerpts from *The Seven Storey Mountain* by Thomas Merton, copyright © 1948 by Harcourt Brace Jovanovich, Inc., and renewed 1976 by The Trustees of the Merton Legacy Trust and from *The Sign of Jonas* by Thomas Merton, copyright © 1953 by the Abbey of Our Lady of Gethsemani and renewed 1981 by The Trustees of the Merton Legacy Trust, reprinted by permission of Harcourt Brace Jovanovich, Inc., and the Society for Promoting Christian Knowledge (SPCK), London. Excerpts from *The Asian Journal of Thomas Merton*, copyright © 1968, 1970, 1973 by The Trustees of the Merton Legacy Trust, and from *The Wisdom of the Desert*, copyright © 1960 by the Abbey of Gethsemani, Inc., reprinted by permission of New Directions Publishing Corporation and SPCK. Excerpts from *The Way of Chuang Tzu* by Thomas Merton, copyright © 1965 by the Abbey of Gethsemani, reprinted by permission of New Directions Publishing Corporation. Selections from *Cables to the Ace* and *The Collected Poems of Thomas Merton*, copyright © 1944, 1968 by Our Lady of Gethsemani, Inc., 1946, 1948 by New Directions Publishing Corporation, reprinted by permission of New Directions Publishing Corporation and Laurence Pollinger Ltd. Excerpts from *Raids on the Unspeakable* by Thomas Merton, copyright © 1966 by the Abbey of Gethsemani, Inc., reprinted by permission of New Directions Publishing Corporation and Burns & Oates Ltd. Excerpts from *New Seeds of Contemplation* by Thomas Merton, copyright © 1961 by The Abbey of Gethsemani, Inc., reprinted by permission of New Directions Publishing Corporation and The Trustees of the Merton Legacy Trust. Excerpts from *My Argument With the Gestapo* by Thomas Merton © 1969 by The Abbey of Gethsemani, Inc., used by permission of Doubleday, a division of Bantam Doubleday Dell Publishing Group Inc., and Laurence Pollinger Ltd. Excerpts from *Conjectures of a Guilty Bystander* by Thomas Merton, copyright © 1965, 1966 by The Abbey of Gethsemani reprinted by permission of Doubleday, a division of Bantam Doubleday Dell Publishing Group, Inc. Excerpts from *Faith and Violence* by Thomas Merton, copyright © 1968 by University of Notre Dame Press reprinted by permission of The Trustees of the Merton Legacy Trust. Excerpts from "Day of the Stranger" by Thomas Merton © 1967 by The Trustees of the Merton Legacy Trust, first published in *The Hudson Review*, Vol, XX, No. 2, Summer 1967, are reprinted by permission of The Trustees of the Merton Legacy Trust. Excerpts from *The Hidden Ground of Love* by Thomas Merton, copyright © 1985 by the Merton Legacy Trust, from *The Road to Joy* by Thomas Merton, copyright © 1989 by the Merton Legacy Trust, and from *A Vow of Conversation*, copyright © 1988 by the Merton Legacy Trust, reprinted by permission of Farrar, Straus & Giroux, Inc., and HarperCollinsPublishers, London. Excerpts from *Love and Living* by Thomas Merton, copyright © 1979 by The Trustees of the Merton Legacy Trust, reprinted by permission of Farrar, Straus & Giroux, Inc. Excerpts from *Seeds of Destruction* by Thomas Merton, copyright © 1964 by the Abbey of Gethsemani, and from *The Secular Journal of Thomas Merton*, copyright © 1959 by Madonna House, reprinted by permission of Farrar, Straus & Giroux, Inc., and the Merton Legacy Trust.

**Library of Congress Cataloging-in-Publication Data**

Forest, James H.
    Living with wisdom : a life of Thomas Merton / Jim Forest.
        p.   cm.
    ISBN 0-88344-755-X
    1. Merton, Thomas, 1915-1968.   2. Trappists — United States —
Biography.   I. Title.
BX4705.M5F67   1991
271'.12502 — dc20
    [B]                                                    91-21922
                                                             CIP

to

*Thomas Hendrickson Hassler-Forest*

*We have what we seek.*
*We don't have to rush after it.*
*It was there all the time,*
*and if we give it time*
*it will make itself known to us.*

—Thomas Merton

John Howard Griffin

*. . . if you want to identify me,*
*ask me not where I live,*
*or what I like to eat,*
*or how I comb my hair,*
*but ask me what I am living for,*
*in detail,*
*and ask me what I think*
*is keeping me from living fully*
*for the thing I want to live for.*

—Thomas Merton

# Contents

# Preface

Thomas Merton entered my life through the pages of his autobiography. I was on Christmas leave from the Navy, waiting in a New York City bus terminal, when I found a paperback copy of *The Seven Storey Mountain* for sale at the news stand. The story of a man who had become a monk seized my interest immediately. In the bus going up the Hudson Valley, I would occasionally look up from the text to gaze out the window at the heavy snow that was falling that night. Merton's story has ever since been linked in my mind with the silent ballet that snow makes during its brief, swirling passage through street lights.

The book played its part in my leaving the Navy eighteen months later as a conscientious objector, though there were many other factors, not least my contact with the Catholic Worker movement. It was to the Catholic Worker house in New York City that I moved after my discharge, and it was there that a more intimate connection with Merton began.

The Catholic Worker's founder, Dorothy Day, was one of Merton's correspondents. She knew of my interest both in monasticism and Merton and encouraged me to write him. My first letter to him had to do with a poem, "Chant to Be Used Around a Site for Furnaces," that Merton had sent Dorothy and which she passed along to me. Merton responded with a letter that was partly about recognizing that we live in a time of war and the need "to shut up and be humble and stay put and trust in God and hope for a peace that we can use for the good of our souls."

Though I didn't know it at the time, that one sentence revealed a great deal about the long-term struggles in which Merton was engaged. I thought what he said was aimed at me (how apt the advice was), but, as was often the case in his letters, he was addressing himself as well. He had enormous difficulty shutting up, feared he was lacking in humility, and often resisted staying put.

Merton thrived on correspondence; there are file cases full of his letters at the Thomas Merton Study Center at Bellarmine College in Louisville, Kentucky. Three collections of his letters have now been published, and more are planned. Merton had such a gift for correspondence that Evelyn Waugh once advised him "to put books aside and write serious letters and make an art of it." Letters were a place to be in touch with others, to think aloud without having to worry about censors, to learn from correspondents, to help and encourage people he cared about, and to offer and receive love. From 1961 until his death seven years later, we exchanged many letters; the correspondence would easily fill a decent-sized book.

Merton often answered letters he received from young people. I suspect he enjoyed glimpsing qualities in them they didn't see in themselves, and helping them find their way. For me, at least, he was a real confessor, even if we were without a confessional.

My original idea of Merton was formed by *The Seven Storey Mountain*, published like all his early books without an author photo, thus making him something of a monk in an iron mask. As can easily happen with a first reading of any book, there was much about the author I missed or misunderstood. Overlooking his sense of humor, I imagined Merton to be an austere sort of person, thin as a rake due to more or less continual fasting, producing a body to match Ichabod Crane's (though I knew Gethsemani was no Sleepy Hollow). The scarecrow image didn't disturb me. Isn't that the way monks are supposed to be? What won me to Merton was not his imagined appearance but his narrative gift and the passion with which he described his steps toward conversion. In a sense, the book was a young man's love letter, the object of his love in this case being not a certain woman, but God, Jesus, Mary, the saints, the Catholic Church, the Trappist Order he had joined, and his particular monastery. Rather off-handedly, everything else was dismissed, including every other variety of Christianity. One could easily get the impression that the best path to heaven was the Trappist high wire. But then love letters are like that: *You* are uniquely beautiful, *you* are the great joy, you and you alone give me a reason to breathe. . . .

Early in our correspondence Merton suggested I come down to visit him. I was able to do so in February 1962. I had no money for the trip—at the Catholic Worker one received room and board plus small change for minor expenses, subway rides and the like. I never dared ask even for small change, preferring to sell *The Catholic Worker* on street corners, keeping some of the proceeds for incidentals. Another companion on the Catholic Worker staff, Bob Kaye, joined me. We decided to travel by thumb. At dawn one damp winter day we loaded up on Italian bread still warm from the oven of the Spring Street bakery and set off for Kentucky. It took two days to reach the Abbey of Gethsemani.

After the Guest Master showed me my room, my first stop was the monastery church. Surviving the exhausting trip, a prayer of thanksgiving came easily. But prayer was cut short by the sound of distant laughter so intense and pervasive that I couldn't resist looking for its source. I hadn't expected laughter at a penitential Trappist monastery.

It originated, I discovered, in Bob Kaye's room, immediately next to mine in the guest house. As I opened the door the laughter was still going on, a kind of gale of joy. Well, I thought, that's the difference between Bob and me. No doubt God prefers devout laughter to pious prayer. Although Bob was laughing, the major source was the red-

faced man on the floor, his feet in the air, hands clutching his belly, knees near his hands. He was wearing black and white robes and a broad leather belt. A shade more well-fed than the fast-chastened Trappist monks I imagined, he reminded me of David Duncan's photos of Pablo Picasso. The man on the floor, laughing with an abandon I had never experienced before, was Thomas Merton. (The inspiration for the laughter? The remarkable smell of feet kept in shoes all the way from the Lower East Side to Gethsemani.)

After that week-long stay at Gethsemani, *The Seven Storey Mountain* was a new and different book. Ever after I was aware that the man writing these books, no matter what the topic, occasionally produced laughter that came directly from heaven.

As anyone will appreciate who has read his autobiographical writing, there were long periods in Merton's life in which laughter must have been rare. Not all his pain had to do with pre-monastic events. Having become the most celebrated monk alive, and the most famous Trappist, it was by no means clear to him that he was in the right place.

When we met in 1962, these matters had largely, but not entirely, been resolved. Merton had achieved a rare degree of freedom and at-homeness with himself. This achievement was certainly not built on his having burned the bridges of connection with the world beyond the monastery. Rather it had to do with realizing the connection between the monk and the world. One of the reasons we were so often in correspondence, and the reason I returned to the monastery two years later for another visit, was because of Merton's concern about religious response to injustice and warfare.

It would be impossible to write a book about Merton without giving attention to his involvement in the peace movement. Yet one of the dangers of having known Merton through a common preoccupation is the temptation to overstress that interest while ignoring or slighting others. I hope this biography comes reasonably close to getting the balance right.

Whatever other labels one might apply to him — essayist, social critic, ecumenical explorer, poet, photographer, artist, correspondent — Merton was primarily a monk. He spent far more time at Mass, in prayer, and in meditation than in writing books and letters or doing anything else likely to bring him to public attention. For much of his life as a monk, he carried various time-consuming responsibilities within the community. There was also the customary physical labor of the community in which he participated along with everyone else. The ordinary substance of life is what is inevitably most neglected in biography; the stress is put on events rather than "non-events." But Merton was mainly interested in the latter.

Inevitably a book of this size neglects much that was important in his life and writing. Nothing will please me more than to know that this book helped open the door to Merton's own writing and, perhaps, to some of the other books about him. There is a partial list of titles in the back of this book.

This present work had its beginning twelve years ago with a smaller book written, at Don Brophy's suggestion, for the Paulist Press. This new edition, suggested by Robert Ellsberg, editor-in-chief for Orbis, is rewritten and greatly expanded. My thanks to him not only for publishing the new book but for his work on the manuscript, as well as to Joan Marie Laflamme, who copy-edited it.

Among others I must thank, my greatest debt is to Michael Mott. His Bible-sized biography, *The Seven Mountains of Thomas Merton*, remains the most complete Merton biography. Thanks also to Bob Lax for his friendship and gentle presence; to Robert Giroux, James Laughlin, and Naomi Burton Stone for various Merton books they have sent me over the years; to Msgr. William Shannon for much advice and encouragement, and the insights in his book on Merton's spirituality, *Thomas Merton's Dark Path*; to Dom John Eudes Bamberger for his essay on Merton and Eastern Orthodoxy; to Sister Donna Kristoff for her essay on Merton and icons; to Brother Patrick Hart for many years of friendship and helpful response to questions about Merton; to Robert Daggy, director of the Merton Studies Center in Louisville, for his assistance over many years and for his help with photos in this book; to Robert O'Nell at Boston College and Kenneth Lohf at Columbia University for their help with photos; to Margot Muntz and Bob

Grip, who helped find errors in the manuscript; and finally to my wife, Nancy, my companion in prayer, writing, reading, and parenthood.

JF
January 20, 1991
Alkmaar, Holland

# Pax Intrantibus

**H**idden away in the hills of Kentucky, a region America knows best for its sour-mash whiskey and purebred horses, is a Trappist monastery.

Unlike the graceful old abbeys in Europe, no one visits the Abbey of Our Lady of Gethsemani to admire the stonework or gaze at the architecture. The collection of stone and brick buildings could hardly be plainer. The inhabitants, once you adjust to their black and white robes, are similarly plain. It is the life they lead that is astonishing.

In the days of Latin liturgy, there were two Latin words painted over the monastery gateway: *Pax intrantibus*. Peace to all who enter. The words were well established in that location on December 10, 1941, when an inconspicuous man with a bland face and sandy hair arrived from New York.

Thomas Merton must have read the words over the gateway with a fine sense of irony. Gleeful man that he could be on solemn occasions, perhaps he laughed. It was only three days since the Japanese attack on America's Pacific fleet at Pearl Harbor and only two days since America's entry into World War II. Lines of young men were waiting their turn at thousands of draft and recruiting offices, over the doors of which another Latin motto could appropriately have been painted: *Bellum intrantibus*. War to all who enter.

Here he was, marching off like so many others, but by himself, out of step, and in the wrong direction.

Many of his compatriots would have found his

Opposite:
The gateway to the Abbey of Gethsemani as it was in 1940. (Photograph courtesy of the Abbey of Gethsemani Archives)

approach to such a gateway a scandalous sight. A
coward, obviously. A man indifferent to Nazi armies
and exploding homes. But an unlined face can be
misleading, and a monastery is rarely an escape
hatch. The young Merton was not unaware or on
the run. He was well-acquainted with the streets of
London, now pitted with bomb craters. For years,
awareness of the war in Europe and its horrors had
eaten away at his soul as acid rain chews limestone.
The peace he sought in the monastery wasn't safe
seclusion. He had come to the Abbey of Gethsemani
partly because he was convinced that the places
where prayer is the main business of life are not at
the edge of history but at the center, and that he
could do more for peace from here than on any battlefield. He was at the monastery gate for the same
reason others were signing up as soldiers: to put his
life on the line.

But there were other aspects to his motives.
Unlike many who were marching off to battle, he
believed that there was little the world treasures that
was worthwhile. From volunteer work in Harlem, he
knew about slums and the human face of racism.
After years of being an outsider in France, England,
and America, he felt little connection with flags.
The world's clamor had made many deaf to conscience. He longed to leave the noise behind, even
the noise of his own typewriter with which he had
previously sought to tap out an identity. He wanted
to leave behind his name and every claim to a place
in the world.

Much that he came for, he found: a silent and
austere life; a life of prayer and worship; a community trying to live for God. But not anonymity. In
less than a decade, Merton's writings would be
talked about from soup kitchens to the papal apart-
ments in the Vatican. His autobiography and a
parade of other books, translated into many languages, would be read not only by Catholics and
other Christians but by Jews, Buddhists, Hindus,

Muslims, and many with no religious labels. His writing would occasion conversion for thousands of readers.

Exactly twenty-seven years later he would die, on the other side of the planet but still a monk of this abbey, by then not only famous but controversial. His essays on war and racism would have brought accusations that he was a Communist disguised in monastic robes. For a time his monastic superiors would have silenced him, though vindications followed, among them gifts from two popes and publication by one of them, John XXIII, of an encyclical that could have been written by Merton: *Pacem in Terris* (*Peace on Earth*). In that decade of assassinations, some would say his death wasn't an accident but murder, and blame it on the CIA.

*Pax Intrantibus.*

The young Merton rang the bell and waited. An old monk showed his face. "I want to be a monk," said the visitor from New York.

Left:
Thomas Merton with "Aunt Kit," his father's sister, during a surprise visit to Gethsemani in 1961. (Photograph courtesy of Boston College, Burns Library)

# Childhood

*Mother wanted me to be independent, and not to run with the herd.*

Thomas Merton was born during a snowstorm late on the last day of January 1915 in Prades, a sheltered town in the French Pyrenees near the Spanish border. It was and remains a place of beauty. Two days' travel away, the First World War had just begun.

His parents had met in 1911 as art students in Paris. Both in their mid-twenties, Ruth Jenkins had grown up in the American Midwest, Owen Merton in New Zealand. They married in London in April 1914, two months before their move to Prades.

It was an artist's attraction to southern light, inexpensive living, and the presence of friends nearby that had brought the Mertons to Prades, but in the summer of 1916 the war chased them to America to take shelter in the home of Ruth's parents, Sam and Martha Jenkins. The house was in Douglaston, Long Island, a commuter ride from Sam's editorial offices in Manhattan. That fall Owen and Ruth rented a dilapidated four-room house in Flushing, Queens, five miles from Douglaston. Two of the rooms were "barely larger than closets."[1]

Recognition of Owen Merton's talent was slowly increasing. His painting, his son later wrote from the monastery, expressed a vision of the world that was "sane, full of balance, full of veneration for structure, for the relations of masses and for all the circumstances that impress an individual identity on

Opposite:
Thomas Merton, age four, as photographed by his mother. (Photograph courtesy of Boston College, Burns Library)

"*I was nobody's dream child. I have seen a diary Mother was keeping, in the time of my infancy and first childhood, and it reflects some astonishment at the stubborn and seemingly spontaneous development of completely unpredictable features in my character, things she had never bargained for: for example, a deep and serious urge to adore the gas-light in the kitchen, with no little ritualistic veneration, when I was about four. Churches and formal religion were things to which Mother attached not too much importance in the training of a modern child . . . *"
(The Seven Storey Mountain)

[5]

each created thing." His vision "was religious and clean."[2] But Owen's sales were rare and the family often lived close to destitution. Ruth's father was well off and eager to help, but Ruth and Owen's pride allowed no familial philanthropy. Owen worked as a gardener, was the organist at a nearby church, and played the piano at a local movie theater in the days before sound tracks.

Tom's parents held radical convictions, among them dedication to simple living and pacifism. Owen had no intention of getting fitted for a uniform and learning how to use a bayonet. Immune to the recruiting posters, military songs, and rhetoric about the "war to end all war," he continued to paint, though he found America did little to bring his brushes to life. Ruth had become a Quaker and on Sundays went to the Friends Meeting House where she was certain not to hear any words of praise for war.

Though Ruth had given up painting, her artist's eye is apparent in photos she took of Tom. In one of them he is sitting in a child's chair, using the seat of an adult chair as a desk. The photo has an icon quality: life haloed in light.

What appealed to her most about Tom was what she recorded in such photos — an early reader capable of intense concentration. But often she found him a difficult, stubborn child who failed to meet her expectations. "Mother wanted me to be independent, and not to run with the herd. I was to be original, individual, I was to have a definite character and ideals of my own. I was not to be an article thrown together, on the common bourgeois pattern, on everybody else's assembly line."[3] Merton remembered her as a "slight, thin, sober little person with a serious and somewhat anxious and very sensitive face . . . worried, precise, quick, critical," a mother of "insatiable dreams and of great ambition after perfection,"[4] which he couldn't, or wouldn't, live up to. His mother sent him to bed early, at age 5, for refus-

Opposite:
Ruth Jenkins Merton. (Photograph courtesy of the Thomas Merton Studies Center)

*"My mother was an American. I have seen a picture of her as a rather slight, thin, sober little person with a serious and somewhat anxious and very sensitive face. And this corresponds with my memory of her — worried, precise, quick, critical of me, her son."*
(The Seven Storey Mountain)

Below:
Merton with his mother. (Photograph courtesy of the Thomas Merton Studies Center)

*"Mother wanted me to be independent, and not to run with the herd. I was to be original, individual, I was to have a definite character and ideals of my own. I was not to be an article thrown together, on the common bourgeois pattern, on everybody's assembly line."*
(The Seven Storey Mountain)

ing to spell *which* with an h. "In the natural order, perhaps solitaries are made by severe mothers," he noted later in life.[5]

Tom's younger brother, John Paul, born November 2, 1918, was more placid. "Everyone was impressed by his constant and unruffled happiness," Merton remembered, without his older brother's "obscure drives and impulses."[6]

Owen Merton was the more serene of Tom's parents. "He was a man of exceptional intellectual honesty and sincerity and purity of understanding," wrote Merton from the monastery, "a man with a wonderful mind and a great talent and a great heart." He took no interest in spelling but, like Ruth, wanted to keep Tom's mind "uncontaminated by error and mediocrity and ugliness and sham."[7]

In the summer of 1921 doctors discovered that Ruth had cancer of the stomach. In October, on her deathbed in a New York hospital, she wrote Tom to say good-bye. Apparently she couldn't bear that he see her in her last condition. "I took the note out

Left:
Owen Merton. (Photograph courtesy of Boston College, Burns Library)

*"Of us all, Father was the only one who really had any kind of faith. And I do not doubt that he had very much of it . . . He was a man of exceptional honesty and sincerity and purity of understanding . . . a man with a wonderful mind and a great talent and a great heart: and what was more, he was the man who had brought me into the world, and had nourished me and cared for me and had shaped my soul and to whom I was bound by every possible kind of bond of affection and attachment and admiration and reverence: killed by a growth on his brain."*
(The Seven Storey Mountain)

under the maple tree in the backyard," Merton remembered, "and worked over it, until I made it all out, and had gathered what it really meant. And a tremendous weight of sadness and depression settled on me."[8] Soon after, her body cremated, there was nothing left of her but some heavy locks of red hair clipped when she was a child, now folded away in tissue paper, and her two sons: Tom, age 6, and John Paul, 3.

Both children moved in with Ruth's parents in Douglaston while Owen, dropping his odd jobs, went travelling. Before long Tom began to accompany his father on travels that took them first to Cape Cod and then to Bermuda, not yet trampled by tourism. Owen not only felt at home in the Caribbean light but fell in love with a novelist, Evelyn Scott. She was married to another artist, Owen's friend Cyril Kay Scott; a *ménage à trois* developed that lasted for nearly two years. A factor in its eventual collapse was Tom's antipathy for Evelyn Scott. "Little Tom *hated* me," she confided.[9]

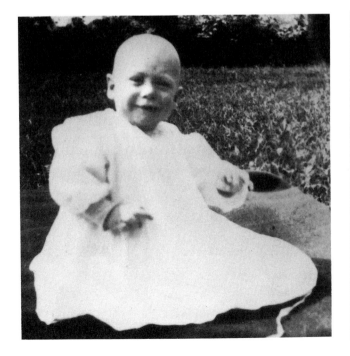

Left:
Thomas Merton in his infancy at Prades, in the French Pyrenees. (Photograph courtesy of the Thomas Merton Studies Center)

*"On the last day of January 1915, under the sign of the Water Bearer, in a year of a great war, and down in the shadow of some French mountains on the borders of Spain, I came into the world. Free by nature, in the image of God, I was nevertheless a prisoner of my own violence and my own selfishness, in the image of the world into which I was born."*

(The Seven Storey Mountain)

Owen Merton's bohemian freedom was shared with Tom. While John Paul was going to school, his older brother was combing beaches and listening to sailors' jokes and stories. "It is almost impossible to make much sense out of the continual rearrangement of our lives and our plans from month to month in my childhood," Merton reflected in adulthood. "Sometimes I had to go to school, sometimes I did not. Sometimes Father and I were living together, sometimes I was with strangers and only saw him from time to time. People came into our lives and went out of our lives. We had now one set of friends, now another. Things were always changing." He briefly attended school on Bermuda and then, without parental objection, dropped out, preferring sand dunes to blackboards. "I could run where I pleased, and do whatever I liked, and life was very pleasant."[10] It was only in 1923, when Owen's travels took him to France and then North Africa, that Tom was left in Douglaston.

"Pop" Jenkins, Tom's grandfather, worked at the publishing company of Grosset & Dunlap, a place that smelled of typewriters and paper. With its shelves of children's books, it seemed to Tom nearly as good a place to be as Bermuda.

Pop Jenkins loved the movies, a passion he passed on to his grandchildren. He had friends in Hollywood. Talk of the private lives of the stars featured at the table of the Jenkins household. In those days Long Island was second only to Hollywood as a center of movie making. At the Bayside Studios near Douglaston, Tom watched Gloria Swanson play the bride in a gypsy wedding scene. But comedy was more to his taste. Take after take, Tom witnessed W. C. Fields stagger down the steps of a tumbledown house, blunder through the bushes, and finally land on top of two cows.

While Sam and Martha Jenkins belonged to the local Episcopal church, Pop's views on religion, as far as Tom could make out, had mainly to do with

*"Mother's death had made one thing evident: Father now did not have to do anything but paint. He was not tied down to any one place. He could go wherever he needed to go, to find subjects and get ideas, and I was old enough to go with him."*

(The Seven Storey Mountain)

what he wasn't: a Catholic or a Jew. Catholics, said Pop, were hypocrites and crooks, and Jews were nearly as bad. *Vatican* was a swear word.

An event that provided one of Merton's most haunting childhood memories occurred in Douglaston when he was 8. As the older brother, Tom was regarded with awe by John Paul, but for Tom the younger brother was a competitor and nuisance. One day Tom and two friends made a hut of scrap lumber and tar paper in the woods, a strictly private preserve off limits to kid brothers. Stones were hurled at nonmembers who dared venture too close. A quarter century later, after subsequent events had sharpened the poignancy of the memory, Merton still recalled John Paul standing in a field a hundred yards away, "a little perplexed 5-year-old kid in short pants and a kind of a leather jacket, standing quite still, with his arms hanging down at his sides, and gazing in our direction, afraid to come any nearer on account of the stones, as insulted as he was saddened, his eyes full of indignation and sorrow. And yet he does not go away . . . his tremendous desire to be with us and to do what we are doing will not permit him to go away. The law written in his nature says that he must be with his elder brother, and do what he is doing: and he cannot understand why this law of love is being so wildly and unjustly violated in his case."[11]

Early in 1925, after the collapse of his relationship with Evelyn and a grave illness he had contracted in Algeria, Owen Merton had an exhibition of his paintings in London. Suddenly his work was being praised by such critics as Roger Fry. Owen returned to Douglaston with money, a beard, and an aura of triumph. After a few months in the Jenkins household, Owen decided the time was ripe for a return to France, taking Tom but leaving John Paul—deemed too young—in Douglaston. It must have been a hard blow for John Paul, far worse than being excluded from Tom's clubhouse. In August Owen and Tom set sail.

Above:
Young Tom. (Photograph courtesy of the Thomas Merton Studies Center)

The new Merton home was in St. Antonin, forty miles above Toulouse in the south of France, a well-preserved medieval town whose geography and architecture still bore witness to an earlier age of faith.

"The town itself," Merton remembered, "was a labyrinth of narrow streets, lined by old thirteenth century houses, mostly falling into ruin. . . . There was nothing left of the color and gaiety and noise of the Middle Ages. Nevertheless, to walk through those streets was to be in the Middle Ages."[12]

The point of convergence was the church. It dominated the town, and from its tower the Angelus bells rang out each day "reminding people of the Mother of God who watched over them."[13] The church and even the countryside beyond the town walls seemed to announce: "This is the meaning of all created things: we have been made for no other purpose than that men may use us in raising themselves to God, and in proclaiming the glory of God."[14]

In the mountains the two Mertons occasionally wandered in the ruins of monasteries, refreshed by "those clean, ancient stone cloisters, those low and mightily rounded arches hewn and set in place by monks."

There were also human embodiments of faith, especially a Catholic family—the Privats, solid Auvergne peasants of Celtic descent—with whom Tom and Owen stayed during the summer of 1927. Merton remembered them for their kindness, their goodness, their peacefulness, their simplicity, and their devout silence about things sacred. Once, trying to prod them into defending their Catholic faith, he told them that the difference between one religion and another was no more significant than different methods of learning arithmetic. All he could get from Monsieur Privat was a quiet and sad sentence, *"Mais c'est impossible."* Merton eventually came to regard the Privats as saints, not canonized church heroes but the invisible kind sanctified by leading ordinary lives in a God-centered way. They were "among the most remarkable people I ever knew."[15] Their home smelled of heaven. Their anxious concern for his soul made him aware that he had one. It was late in life that Tom discovered the reason for his long stay with the Privats: a doctor in St. Antonin had discovered Tom had tuberculosis. The Privats had agreed to help provide the rest and care needed to nurse him back to health.[16]

If the Privat home had the peace of heaven, the boarding school Tom was sent to in Montauban, twenty-five miles to the southwest, more closely resembled hell: a fiercely secular environment in which to hard boil the brain. Twenty years later Merton regarded such schools as typical. "Is it any wonder that there can be no peace in a world where everything possible is done to guarantee that the youth of every nation will grow up absolutely without moral and religious discipline, and without the shadow of an interior life, or of that spirituality and

Above:
Thomas Merton with his younger brother, John Paul. (Photograph courtesy of the Thomas Merton Studies Center)

*"I suppose it is usual for elder brothers, when they are still children, to feel themselves demeaned by the company of a brother four or five years younger, whom they regard as a baby and whom they tend to patronise and look down upon."*

(The Seven Storey Mountain)

charity and faith which alone can safeguard the treaties and agreements made by governments?"[17]

Nonetheless Tom learned. He was speaking French like a native, including many words never used in print. In his autobiography he accused the Lycée of being an academy of flippancy and cynicism, but later in life, no longer needing to see his past in such black-and-white terms, he fondly remembered Monsieur Delmas, a teacher who had introduced him to the writings of Fénelon.[18] It was while there that Tom Merton began to see himself as a writer. He found a circle "of more or less peaceful friends" who had "more wit than obscenity about them. . . . They had ideals and ambitions and, as a matter of fact, by the middle of the first year, I remember we were all furiously writing novels."[19]

It was during those three years in France that Tom began to glimpse his father's religious faith. "I shall never forget," he wrote in *The Seven Storey Mountain*, "a casual remark Father happened to make in which he told me of St. Peter's betrayal of Christ, and how, on hearing the cock crow, Peter went out and wept bitterly. . . . We were just talking casually, standing in the hall of the flat we had taken. . . . I have never lost the vivid picture I got, at that moment, of Peter going out and weeping bitterly."[20]

He recalled on another occasion his father's indignation with a woman speaking hatefully of a neighbor. "He asked her why she thought Christ had told people to love their enemies. Did she suppose God commanded this for His benefit? Did he get anything out of it that he really needed from us? Or was it rather for our own good that he had given us this commandment? He told her that if she had any sense, she would love other people if only for the sake of the good and health and peace of her own soul."[21]

*"The only really valuable religious and moral training I ever got as a child came to me from my father, not systematically, but here and there and more or less spontaneously, in the course of ordinary conversations. Father never applied himself, of set purpose, to teach me religion. But if something spiritual was on his mind, it came out more or less naturally."*

(The Seven Storey Mountain)

# England

*I believe in nothing.*

Owen Merton arrived in Montauban one day in May 1928 to withdraw Tom from class and give him the news that they were moving to England. An exhibition of his paintings was being mounted in London. Owen had reluctantly decided that there were better prospects in Britain for both father and son. Leaving France was a defeat for Owen but a liberation for his 13-year-old son. No more Lycée! "How the light sang on the brick walls of the prison whose gates had just burst open before me."[22]

Aunt Maud and Uncle Ben had invited them to live in their red brick house, "a fortress of nineteenth-century security"[23] in Ealing, West London. For Tom the house's great treasure was his elderly Aunt Maud—Maud Grierson Pearce, sister of Owen's mother—a sprightly and meek lady who dressed as if Queen Victoria's Diamond Jubilee had occurred only yesterday. Her pointed nose and her thin smiling lips suggested the expression of one who had just finished pronouncing, "How nice!"[24]

Shortly after their arrival Tom confided to Aunt Maud his hope of becoming a writer. "What sort of writing," she asked. "Stories," he said. "No doubt you could do that quite well," Maud assured him, "but you ought to keep in mind that writers often find it difficult to pay their bills. Perhaps you could be a journalist as well?" Merton agreed. "A foreign correspondent?" she suggested. "Perhaps," he said.

Tom's schooling resumed at Ripley Court in Sur-

*"Then, after that, the channel steamer, Folkestone cliffs, white as cream in the sunny haze, the jetty, the grey-green downs and the line of prim hotels along the top of the rock: these things all made me happy. And the cockney cries of the porters and the smell of strong tea in the station refreshment room spelled out all the associations of what had, up to now, always been a holiday country for me, a land heavy with awe-inspiring proprieties, but laden with all kinds of comforts, and in which every impact of experience seemed to reach the soul through seven or eight layers of insulation."*

(The Seven Storey Mountain)

[15]

rey. The headmistress was Aunt Maud's sister-in-law. He felt at home with chapel prayer and Anglican ritual, finding "many occasions of praying and lifting up my mind to God." It was "the first time I had ever seen people kneel publicly by their beds before getting into them, and the first time I had ever sat down to meals after a grace. . . . For about the next two years I think I was almost sincerely religious."[25] In his autobiography, however, perhaps looking back too critically, he regarded his adolescent sojourn in the Church of England less as an experience of sacramental life than an exploration of English social tradition.

Tom's major academic project at Ripley Court was to acquire enough Latin to make a decent showing in scholarship exams for public school. There were hopes in the family that, despite his bohemian origins, Tom might be accepted at an elite school like Harrow. Sam Jenkins, his grandfather in America, was prepared to pick up the tab. But in the end Oakham was selected, "an obscure but decent little school in the Midlands," seventy miles northwest of London in Oakham.[26]

In the shelter and tranquility of Ripley Court life had seemed as secure as Hobbiton in Tolkien's mythical Middle Earth. Then, while on Scottish summer holiday in 1929 with his father, Tom's world collapsed once more. Owen was suddenly taken ill. Doctors discovered a malignant brain tumor. His life was at risk and his sanity affected. "ENTERING NEW YORK HARBOR. ALL WELL," said a telegram Owen sent to Tom from a London hospital.

At Oakham that fall Tom read Chaucer's *Canterbury Tales* and labored over Greek verbs in the shadow of his father's tumor. The chapel life that had blossomed for him at Ripley Court abruptly perished. Merton later credited this partly to the school chaplain, a man who liked to insert the word *gentleman* into biblical texts. The first verse of chapter 13 of First Corinthians became: "If I talk with the tongues of men and angels, and be not a gentleman, I am become as sounding brass." This celebration of correct manners had nothing to offer the son of a man whose father was on his deathbed.

"St. Peter and the other Apostles would have been rather surprised," Merton wrote as a monk, "at the concept that Christ had been scourged and beaten by soldiers, cursed and crowned with thorns and subjected to unutterable contempt and finally nailed to the Cross and left to bleed to death in order that we might all become gentlemen."[27]

In the chapel Tom kept a tight-lipped silence when other students recited the Creed. His counter-creed was "I believe in nothing."

Meanwhile, Sam Jenkins was doing all he could to make practical provisions for his grandsons. When he came to England in the summer of 1930 to explain what he had arranged, Tom was astonished

Left:
Oakham, the English public school where Merton was enrolled. (Photograph courtesy of Oakham School)

*"Oakham, Oakham! The grey murk of the winter evenings in that garret where seven or eight of us moiled around in the gaslight, among the tuck-boxes, noisy, greedy, foul-mouthed, fighting and shouting!"*

(The Seven Storey Mountain)

to find himself the possessor of stock in Grosset &
Dunlap, the owner of land on Long Island, and, with
John Paul, possessor of Stone Island off the coast of
Maine. On top of this, there would be an allowance
for Tom from now on, to be dispensed by Tom's
godfather, Dr. Thomas Bennett in London. Bennett,
a family friend, was in charge of Owen's treatment;
he later became Tom's guardian. Wanting to offer
Tom a symbol of passage into the adult world, Pop
Jenkins presented the 15-year-old Tom with a pipe
and a pouch of St. Julian tobacco.

Tom's residence when away from school was the
Bennett flat at 2 Mandeville Place in London's West
End. A wealthy, cosmopolitan world opened its
doors to Tom. The Bennett's French maid brought
him breakfast in bed. With money jingling in his
pocket, he became a steady customer at many book
shops and began building a significant collection of
jazz records. Whole days were spent at the movies.

"I discovered [as part of the Bennett household]
that one was not only allowed to make fun of English middle-class notions and ideals but encouraged
to do so. . . . I soon developed a habit of wholesale
and glib detraction of all the people with whom I
did not agree or whose taste and ideas offended
me."[28]

In a climate of cultivated sarcasm and refined
open-mindedness, it was hard for Merton to grasp
the fine distinction between behavior that was
admired in books and one's actual behavior. "I did
not see . . . that [the Bennetts'] interest in D. H.
Lawrence as art was, in some subtle way, discon-
nected from any endorsement of his ideas about how
a man ought to live. Or rather, the distinction was
more subtle still . . . it was between their interest in
and amusement at those ideas, and the fact, which
they took for granted, that it was rather vulgar to
practice them the way Lawrence did. This was a distinction which I did not grasp until it was too
late."[29]

*"I sat there in the dark, unhappy room, unable
to think, unable to move, with all the innumer-
able elements of my isolation crowding in upon
me from every side: without a home, without a
family, without a country, without a father,
apparently without any friends, without any
interior peace or confidence or light or understanding of my own — without God, too, without
God, without heaven, without grace, without
anything."*

(The Seven Storey Mountain)

[18]

Surrounding the Bennetts' island of affluence and good taste was the Great Depression, in which many were perishing. The beggars on London's streets gave Tom pause for thought.

It was not only the poor of England who caught his eye. In regard to India, his sympathies were with Gandhi. The Salt March and the campaign that followed it had resulted in the Round Table Conference. Gandhi was in England, providing the British public with the spectacle of a national leader who chose to live in London's slums, refused to eat meat, had a goat in his entourage, and wore next to nothing. He was, for Tom and for all of England, "a small, disquieting question mark."[30] In the fall of 1930, Tom took Gandhi's side in a formal school debate, arguing that India had every right to demand Britain's withdrawal. The opposing view — that the Indians were backward, pagan people, incapable of taking care of themselves — carried the day, 38 to 6.[31]

Owen Merton remained at Middlesex Hospital in London. By the summer of 1930 he was on a bed of silence, a huge lump on his bandaged head and stripped of the ability to speak. Yet Tom discovered his father's eyes were full of recognition and clarity. Tom wept, and Owen wept with him.

Tom saw suffering as "a raw wound for which there was no adequate relief." All that he had heard at chapel services seemed meaningless in the context of war, disease, starvation, and death. "You had to take it, like an animal." Avoid what you can, and numb yourself to the rest. "The truth that many people never understand, until it is too late," he commented later, "is that the one who does the most to avoid suffering is, in the end, the one who suffers most. . . . It is his own existence, his own being, that is at once the subject and the source of his pain, and his very existence and consciousness is his greatest torture."[32]

Within the family, it was only his father who was

Above:
Mahatma Gandhi. (Photograph courtesy of Maryknoll archives)

*"I remember arguing about Gandhi in my school dormitory: chiefly against the football captain, then head prefect . . . I insisted that Gandhi was right . . . Such sentiments were of course beyond comprehension. How could Gandhi be right when he was odd?"*

(Seeds of Destruction)

able to make something of his calamity and was even able to communicate it to Tom despite his excommunication from words. One day Owen was drawing again, expressing in images the events occurring within him. The drawings "were unlike anything he had ever done before—pictures of little, irate Byzantine-looking saints with beards and great halos."[33]

In his months of desperate illness and pain Owen had found his way to pre-Reformation Christianity with its image-centered spirituality, about which no one in the family knew anything. The one thing that was clear to Tom was that his dying father was a religious man. "Behind the walls of his isolation, his intelligence and his will . . . were turned to God, and communed with God." He was finding a way "to understand and make use of his suffering for his own good, and to perfect his soul."[34]

The tiny icons Owen had drawn were his last "words" before entering a deeper silence. On January 18, 1931, just after Tom returned from a Christmas trip to Strasbourg, Owen Merton died. Eleven days short of his sixteenth birthday, Tom was an orphan.

At the time, Tom could make nothing of his father's death. For a couple of months he was sad and depressed. He coped by focusing his considerable energies on study, making rapid headway in languages—Latin, Greek, French, German and Italian—and reading until a pair of reading glasses was needed. During the Easter holiday he managed a brief, inconsequential visit to Rome. It was a solitary trip, as were most of his walks while at school or in London.

He later regarded this period of his life, too severely, as a season of complete flattening. "It was in this year," he remembered, "that the hard crust of my dry soul finally squeezed out all the last traces of religion that had ever been in it. There was no room for any God in that empty temple full of dust and rubbish which I was now so jealously to guard

against all intruders, in order to devote it to the worship of my own stupid will. And so I became the complete twentieth-century man . . . a true citizen of my own disgusting century: the century of poison gas and atomic bombs. A man living on the doorsill of the Apocalypse."[35]

In fact his head wasn't quite as empty as he claimed in the high relief of his autobiography. Among other things, 1931 was the year his love for the poems of William Blake began. Seven years later, Blake became the subject of Merton's graduate studies at Columbia.

That summer Tom travelled to America for a stay with his brother and grandparents, falling intensely in love aboard ship on the way, and on the way back sharing the ship with some detectives, a gangster, a notorious playboy, and a crowd of students from Vassar and Bryn Mawr with whom he ran up a

Above:
Thomas Merton (top row, third from left) with his Oakham rugby team. (Photograph courtesy of Oakham School)

*"There was no rowing at Oakham, since there was no water. But the chaplain had been a rowing 'blue' at Cambridge, in his time. He was a tall, powerful, handsome man, with hair greying at the temples, and a big English chin, and a broad, uncreased brow, with sentences like 'I stand for fair-play and good sportsmanship' written all over it."*

(The Seven Storey Mountain)

sizeable bar bill. "I cannot tell which is the more humiliating," he wrote in his autobiography, "the memory of the half-baked adolescent I was in June or the glib and hard-boiled specimen I was in October when I came back to Oakham."[36]

During his weeks of travel, he decided he was an *ex-officio* Communist. He had read the *Communist Manifesto*, found it more or less agreeable, and for a time kept it on view in his room, a prop indicating that a revolutionary was in residence. Photos of Greco-Roman Venuses took the place of movie star pin-ups. He felt he had at last grown up. "I fancied that I had suddenly risen above all the errors and stupidities and mistakes of modern society—there are enough of these to rise above, I admit—and that I had taken my place in the ranks of those who held up their heads and squared their shoulders and marched into the future." Unfortunately, the "only future we seem to walk into," he remarked in his autobiography, "is full of bigger and more terrible wars, wars well calculated to knock our upraised heads off those squared shoulders."[37] Liberty and independence were key words for him, qualities he exercised in ways that occasionally brought sharp reproofs from Tom Bennett. "I believed in the beautiful myth about having a good time so long as it does not hurt anybody else."[38]

Tom's literary gift having been noticed during the first year, he became editor (and often illustrator) of *The Oakhamian* that fall. It was in that role that he had his first encounter with censorship: a colorful piece he had written about New York City reached print in grayer shades.

*"For it had become evident to me that I was a great rebel. I fancied that I had suddenly risen above all the errors and stupidities and mistakes of modern society . . . and that I had taken my place in the ranks of those who held up their heads and squared their shoulders and marched into the future . . . The only future we seem to walk into, in actual fact, is full of bigger and more terrible wars, wars well calculated to knock our upraised heads off those squared shoulders."*

(The Seven Storey Mountain)

# The Christ of the Icons

*Without knowing anything about it, I became a pilgrim.*

In the spring of 1932 Merton set off to go walking along the Rhine, an excursion that happened to coincide with Hitler's campaign for the German chancellorship. Along the way he witnessed villagers hurling bricks and fighting with pitchforks as political passions spilled over. The trip reached its nadir one morning when, while walking down a quiet country road lined with apple orchards, he was nearly run down by a car full of young Nazis waving their fists.[39] Tom dived into a ditch in the nick of time, the car's occupants showering him with *Wählt Hitler* leaflets as they passed.

Pain in one toe cut the German trip short. While in London Merton didn't bother to ask Tom Bennett to look at it, but by the time he was back at Oakham the soreness got worse. A few days later he found himself hampered not only by his toe but suffering a toothache. The school dentist extracted a tooth, which turned out to be the cork capping an infection that had spread throughout Tom's body. The aching toe proved to be gangrenous. His body was full of poisoned blood.

For weeks he was in a sanitorium, during the first days barely conscious. He expected to die and viewed the prospect with complete apathy. He was later impressed by the fact that it had never occurred to him to pray. Death seemed quite a suitable revenge on life. Merton recovered but took no

Below:
Mosaic of the crucifixion from the Basilica of San Clemente, Rome.

pleasure in it. He was convinced of the ultimate meaninglessness of life.

In the summer he stayed with John Paul and his grandparents in a mammoth hotel in Bournemouth where a summer romance brought on emotional storms and long, solitary walks on the Dorset downs. After that he packed his rucksack and went camping by himself in the New Forest, savoring the nighttime noises of frogs and running water.

In September his examination results arrived. He had won a place at Clare College, Cambridge, to be taken up the following fall. He left Oakham in December, and in February 1933 he set off for an extended holiday in Italy.

What his brush with death hadn't done, Rome did. The 17-year-old Merton began to feel a pulse in his soul and a longing to pray. It was not the usual sights that moved him, neither the "vapid, boring, semi-pornographic statuary of the Empire"[40] nor the ecclesiastical monuments of the Renaissance and Counter-Reformation that he had first sought out as a dutiful tourist reading his Baedeker. Rather, it was the city's most ancient churches.

"I was fascinated by these Byzantine mosaics. I began to haunt the churches where they were to be found, and . . . all the other churches [among them Saints Cosmas and Damian, Santa Maria Maggiore, Santa Sabina, the Lateran, and Santa Costanza] that were more or less of the same period. . . . Without knowing anything about it, I became a pilgrim."[41]

The principal icons were windows through which he felt Christ's gaze. "For the first time in my whole life I began to find out something of who this Person was that men call Christ. . . . It is the Christ of the Apocalypse, the Christ of the Martyrs, the Christ of the Fathers. It is the Christ of St. John, and of St. Paul. . . . It is Christ God, Christ King."[42] (Icons continued to play a vital role in Merton's spiritual life. In letters written in 1967 and 1968, he said that he wasn't drawn to a Christ who was merely a his-

torical figure possessing "a little flash of the light" but to "the Christ of the Byzantine icons" who "represents a traditional experience formulated in a theology of light, the icon being a kind of sacramental medium for the illumination and awareness of the glory of Christ within us. ... What one 'sees' in prayer before an icon is not an external representation of a historical person, but an interior presence in light, which is the glory of the transfigured Christ, the experience of which is transmitted in faith from generation to generation by those who have 'seen,' from the Apostles on down. ... So when I say that my Christ is the Christ of the icons, I mean that he is reached not through any scientific study but through direct faith and the mediation of the liturgy, art, worship, prayer, theology of light, etc., that is all bound up with the Russian and Greek tradition."[43])

D. H. Lawrence's books, previously much valued

by Merton, suddenly seemed to him as shallow as movie posters. Eager to understand iconography, he bought an English translation of the New Testament. Perhaps he remembered his father's efforts to interest him in the Bible when he was ten. "I read more and more of the Gospels, and my love for the old churches and their mosaics grew from day to day." He realized their attraction wasn't simply his appreciation of the aesthetics of iconography but a profound sense of peace he experienced within such walls. He had a "deep and strong conviction that I belonged there."[44] He found this was true even in churches that had no aesthetic attraction for him. "One of my favorite shrines was that of St. Peter in Chains, and I did not love it for any work of art that was there, since the big attraction, the big 'number,' the big 'feature' in that place is Michelangelo's Moses. But I have always been extremely bored by that horned and pop-eyed frown. . . . Perhaps what attracted me to that Church was the Apostle himself to whom it is dedicated."[45]

Below:
St. Peter's Square, the Vatican. (Photograph courtesy of Maryknoll archives)

*"There was something else that attracted me [to the churches of Rome]: a kind of interior peace. I loved to be in these holy places. I had a kind of deep and strong conviction that I belonged there: that my rational nature was filled with profound desires and needs that could only find satisfaction in churches of God."*
(The Seven Storey Mountain)

Alone one night in his *pensione* room on the corner of Via Sistina and Via Tritone, trying to record in his journal his thoughts about Byzantine icons, he sensed his father's presence, "as real and startling as if he had touched my arm or spoken to me." The experience was over in a flash, "but in that flash, instantly, I was overwhelmed with a sudden and profound insight into the misery and corruption of my own soul. . . . And now, I think for the first time in my whole life, I really began to pray . . . praying out of the very roots of my life and my being, and praying to the God I had never known."[46]

Owen Merton's "last words" to his son were his drawings of Byzantine saints. It was in these days of being surrounded by some of the icons surviving from the church's early centuries that Tom felt stricken to tears by the state of his soul and overcome by the need to pray. It was at this moment that he felt his father's closeness.

The next day, still broken by contrition, he visited the Church of Santa Sabina. Once inside, he knew that he had to pray there. It was impossible to play the guidebook-studying tourist any longer. Yet public prayer was intensely embarrassing. All he could manage that first day was to cross himself with blessed water as he entered and to recite the Our Father over and over again as he knelt down at the altar rail. "That day in Santa Sabina, although the church was almost empty, I walked across the stone floor mortally afraid that a poor devout old Italian woman was following me with suspicious eyes."[47] For all his fears, he walked out feeling reborn. His final week in Rome was a time of joy such as he hadn't known in years.

From Italy he went on to the United States for a family visit. He brought his Bible along, but the embarrassment he had felt in trying to pray that first day in Santa Sabina still haunted him. He read the Bible surreptitiously, afraid someone would make fun of him. Nonetheless he began to window-shop for a

Above:
Interior, Basilica of Santa Sabina.

*"I went to the Dominican's Church, Santa Sabina. And it was a very definite experience, something that amounted to a capitulation, a surrender, a conversion, not without struggle, even now, to walk deliberately into the church with no other purpose than to kneel down and pray to God."*

(The Seven Storey Mountain)

[27]

church. Despite the at-homeness he had felt in Roman churches, a long-standing aversion to Catholicism remained. No doubt he was also sensitive to Sam Jenkins's hostility to the Catholic Church. He tried the Zion Episcopal Church, to which Sam and Martha belonged and where his father had once been organist, but the service only irritated him. He next went to a Quaker Meeting in Flushing. His mother had been a Quaker and had meditated there. He enjoyed the silence while it lasted but was annoyed by what one member had to say about the virtues of the Swiss. What had thrilled him in those iconed churches in Rome wasn't here. He didn't return.

The religious awakening in Rome seemed to fade out. In Chicago for the World's Fair, Merton got a job as barker for a strip-tease show called "The Streets of Paris." After the complex sexual reticence of England and the ornate eroticism of France, he found the undisguised and sweaty frankness of the American variety refreshing.

Back in New York, he joined the artist Reg Marsh, a friend of his father's, in making the rounds of burlesque houses in Manhattan and Coney Island — places since immortalized by Marsh's paintings. These were Marsh's cathedrals, where life was coarse but real. Marsh loved to draw the large-eyed, lonely men hungering for the lithesome young women beyond the footlights.

At the summer's end, Merton sailed back to England minus his Bible, his memories of prayer in Rome dormant.

# Cambridge

*Shall I . . . wake up the dirty ghosts?*

Cambridge suggests England at its most attractive: beautifully proportioned classical architecture, dons in medieval academic gowns, young men in straw hats boating on the River Cam along banks crowded with spring daffodils, choirs singing Evensong in cathedrals that seem to have fallen to earth from heaven. But what Merton remembered was the scent of decay during the "nadir of winter darkness."[48]

The bleakest year of his life began with his arrival at Clare College, Cambridge, in October 1933.

Merton found lodgings on Bridge Street. Nearby were two friends from Oakham, Ray Dickens and Andrew Winser. During their first months at Cambridge, ignoring church, the three enjoyed late Sunday morning breakfasts together. By throwing bread crumbs to ducks swimming in the Cam below Dickens's window, they tested Pavlov's theories of conditioned behavior.

Merton quickly acquired quite different companions at Cambridge, many of them listed by the proctor for "conduct unbecoming a gentleman." Anything but tame and shy, these "were the ones who made all the noise when there was a 'bump supper.' We lived in the Lion Inn. We fought our way in and out of 'the Red Cow.' "[49]

In his autobiography Merton asks, "Shall I . . . wake up the dirty ghosts under the trees of the Backs [an area along the Cam behind the colleges], and out beyond the Clare New Building and in

Below:
Clare College, Cambridge. (Photograph by Jim Forest)

*"Perhaps to you the atmosphere of Cambridge is neither dark nor sinister . . . But for me, with my blind appetites, it was impossible that I should not rush in and take a huge bite of this rotten fruit. The bitter taste is still with me after not a few years."*

(The Seven Storey Mountain)

[29]

some rooms down on Chesterton Road?"[50]

He let the ghosts slumber, leaving his readers to wonder what was left unsaid. In fact, Merton was ordered by his superiors to leave out the more scandalous events in his life.[51] One has to recall that in 1948, when *The Seven Storey Mountain* was published, neither *Playboy* nor anything like it was on sale; even works of literature like James Joyce's *Ulysses* were still banned. Merton's readers had to take his word for it that he was guilty of mortal sins "more powerful than any explosive."[52]

November 14, 1933, was a date that haunted Merton for the rest of his life, figuring in poems, journals, and especially his unpublished autobiographical novel, *Labyrinth*, written in 1939. Though the pages describing the main events of that night have disappeared, Merton's friend and literary agent, Naomi Burton, remembers the lost section as describing a drunken party at Cambridge at which one of the students agreed to be nailed to a cross. "In the drunken chaos that followed," writes Michael Mott in describing Burton's recollections, "everything seemed so out of control that the mock crucifixion came close to being a real one."[53] In the text, the narrator is nearly arrested by the Cambridge police.

Circumstantial evidence suggests that what was described in the novel's lost pages actually occurred, and that it happened to Merton. On Merton's United States certificate of naturalization, issued in 1951, the only "visible distinctive mark" listed was a scar on the palm of his right hand. Naomi Burton recalls noticing the scar in the early sixties. With obvious embarrassment, Merton referred to it as his "stigmata."[54]

"There is certainly an odd way in which the word 'crucifixion' clings to [Merton's] references to Cambridge," Mott comments.[55] There is one such passage in Merton's novel, *My Argument with the Gestapo*, where the candles on a church altar seem to say to

*"With every nerve and fibre of my being I was laboring to enslave myself in the bonds of my own intolerable disgust. There is nothing new or strange about the process. But what people do not realize is that this is the crucifixion of Christ: in which He dies again and again in the individuals who were made to share the joy and the freedom of His grace, and who deny Him."*
(The Seven Storey Mountain)

the book's Merton-like protagonist: "Your pride was not the world's fault, but yours, because you were the one who finally consented to be proud. Look now where the Crucifixion flowered in London like a tree, and the wounds were made in Cambridge, red as oleanders."[56]

Merton's poem "The Biography" opens in Cambridge and is about his participation in Christ's suffering and parallel crucifixion:

> Although my life is written in Christ's Body
>     like a map,
> The nails have printed in those open hands
> More than the abstract names of sins,
> More than the counties and the towns,
> The names of streets, the numbers of the
>     houses,
> The record of the days and nights,
> When I have murdered Him in every square
>     and street.
> Lance and thorn, and scourge and nail
> Have more than made His Flesh my
>     chronicle . . .[57]

It was a hellish interval in Merton's life, "an incoherent riot of undirected passion,"[58] said Merton; a time of "beer, bewilderment and sorrow," says his compassionate friend, Bob Lax.[59]

Merton's Aunt Maud died at just this time. "They committed the thin body of my Victorian angel to the clay of Ealing, and buried my childhood with it," he recalled. The England he had once seen through the eyes of her simplicity was buried with her. "I had fallen through the surface of old England into the hell, the vacuum and the horror that London was nursing in her avaricious heart."[60]

Merton had now been orphaned three times over: mother, father, and dearest aunt. He felt more cut off than ever from Christianity. Drinking heavily, he had become one of the more desperate undergradu-

Above:
Thomas Merton's passport photo at the time of his arrival in the United States. (Photograph courtesy of the Thomas Merton Studies Center)

*"God in His mercy was permitting me to fly as far as I could from His love but at the same time preparing to confront me, at the end of it all, and in the bottom of the abyss, when I thought I had gone farthest away from Him."*
(The Seven Storey Mountain)

ates at Cambridge. And he had lost his virginity.

Merton had been reading Freud, Jung, and Adler, struggling to understand, insofar as hangovers allowed, "the mysteries of sex-repression."[61] There was very little sex repression in his life that winter. He later recalled to a friend that his initial sexual experience was with a prostitute he encountered in Hyde Park, London. He claimed to have learned Hungarian in bed. There was a woman he saw from time to time in Cambridge who was known as "the freshman's delight."

In a journal entry written in 1965 he confessed, "I suppose I am the person who lived for a while at 71 Bridge Street, Cambridge. . . . And Clare was my College, and I was a damned fool, sitting on the steps of the boat house late at night with Sylvia."[62]

The details remain hidden, but, whether by Sylvia or someone else, he had inadvertently fathered a child. Later on he told friends that lawyers had been brought in. Tom Bennett apparently arranged a legal settlement with the mother. (There have been rumors that mother and child were killed in the blitz. At least as late as early 1944, however, Merton believed they were alive. A will he wrote that February directs that half his estate should go to Tom Bennett, to be passed on "to the person mentioned to him in my letters, if that person can be contacted."[63])

Bennett's relationship with Merton had been deteriorating for months. Bennett had sent him an irate letter during his Italian sojourn in the summer. Merton had been spending money too carelessly. Because of rowdy late-night behavior when coming down to London from Clare, Tom was no longer welcome at the Bennett flat and had to sleep in a hotel. It was Bennett who had the irksome job of arranging the settlement for Merton's paternity.

Bennett's letters, Merton recalled, "got sharper as they went on, and finally, in March or April, I got a curt summons to come to London." After a long

Below:
71 Bridge Street, where Merton lived for a time in Cambridge. (Photograph by Barry Gardiner)

interval in Bennett's waiting room, Merton was received with "devastating coolness" and told to explain. "My tongue would hardly function. And the words I murmured about my 'making mistakes' and 'not wanting to hurt others' sounded extremely silly and cheap."[64] Apparently Merton never met his guardian again.

During the summer of 1934, while Merton was staying in America at the Jenkins home at Douglaston, Bennett wrote to urge him not to return to England. His academic results at Cambridge hadn't been good enough. He would lose his scholarship. Even if the money needed to keep him at Clare could be found, he had no chance of ever getting into the British diplomatic service. The sensible thing to do, said Bennett, was to stay in America. "It did not take me five minutes to come around to agreeing with him."[65] He felt like B'rer Rabbit being hurled into the briar patch.

For all its calamities, Merton's year at Cambridge wasn't a total loss. Perhaps the high point was Professor Bullough's class on Dante's *Divine Comedy*. Canto by canto, Merton had read his way to the frozen core of hell, at last ascending purgatory toward the warmth of heaven. Merton's initial irritation with the poet's theology gradually had given way to gladness as he followed "the slow and majestic progress of the myths and symbols in which Dante was building up a whole poetic synthesis of scholastic philosophy and theology." Reading Dante was "the one great benefit I got out of Cambridge."[66] It was the *Purgatorio*'s seven storey mountain of painful ascent to heaven that later gave Merton the title for his autobiography.

"Lady, when on that night I left the Island that was once your England, your love went with me, although I could not know it, and could not make myself aware of it. And it was your love, your intercession for me, before God, that was preparing the seas before my ship, laying open the way for me to another country."
(The Seven Storey Mountain)

# New York City

*You found yourself saying excellent things that you did not know you knew, and that you had not, in fact, known before.*

Though his mother had been an American citizen, Tom wasn't. After his summer on Long Island he had to return to England to apply for permission to live in America. Back in London in late October he filled out the forms and got the visa. No reconciliation with Tom Bennett occurred, nor did it happen in later years. On November 29, 1934, Merton left Europe for the last time.

The Europe the 19-year-old Merton abandoned that winter "was a sad and unquiet continent, full of forebodings."[67] It seemed just a matter of time before the wholesale dying began. Merton felt "the cold steel of the war-scare in my vitals."[68]

Taking stock of the events at Cambridge while at sea made him miserably aware that a kind of war was being waged within himself. All he had been trying to do that year was to enjoy himself without hurting anyone. Yet nothing had worked out the way it was supposed to. "Everything I had reached out for turned to ashes in my hands. . . . I myself, into the bargain, had turned out to be an extremely unpleasant sort of person—vain, self-centered, dissolute, weak, irresolute, undisciplined, sensual, obscene and proud. I was a mess." He felt the desperate need to apologize, even to confess, but weighing against that was the conviction that "confession is ill-bred, and embarrassing to everyone concerned in it." After

Opposite:
Thomas Merton as he appeared in the Columbia Yearbook of 1939. (Photograph courtesy of Boston College Library)

*"Externally (I thought) I was a success. Everybody knew who I was at Columbia. Those who had not yet found out, soon did when the Yearbook came out, full of pictures of myself. It was enough to tell them more about me than I intended, I suppose. They did not have to be very acute to see through the dumb self-satisfied expression in all those portraits."*

(The Seven Storey Mountain)

[35]

all, as he later wrote in *My Argument With the Gestapo*, confession implies there is such a thing as sin. "Sin was a morbid concept, and if you had it in your mind, this concept would poison you entirely and you would go crazy."[69]

In the course of a stormy Atlantic crossing, his back to Rome as well as London, Merton toyed with a more rational conversion than had attracted him the day he prayed in Santa Sabina. Religion seemed irrelevant and ridiculous. Marxism, however, was regarded as a kind of practical science. Along with a variety of dissident movements, Merton had identified with Communism, in a vague way, for two years. The Soviet Union was widely reported as a place where an oppressive old regime had been swept aside and a new order set up in which everyone had a fair share and a job: no Great Depression, no evictions, no homeless people sleeping under bridges. Despite press photos he had seen of immense propaganda posters "hanging over the walls of the world's ugliest buildings in Moscow," he had the idea that the Soviet Union was the refuge of "true art" while Europe and America were still in the grip of "bourgeois ugliness." On top of everything else, in the circles Merton was travelling, Communism was in fashion.

Perhaps the most attractive feature of Communism was that it absolved him of personal responsibility for what he had done in Cambridge. "It was not so much I myself that was to blame for unhappiness, but the society in which I lived. . . . I was the product of my times, my society and my class . . . spawned by the selfishness and irresponsibility of the materialistic century in which I lived."[70]

Intellectually pardoned, and determined to turn himself in a new direction, he resolved to devote himself to helping build the new Communist order. "I had my new religion all ready for immediate use"[71] and was primed to enter the fray against capitalism and to clear the ground for the classless soci-

Below:
Statue in Columbia quadrangle. (Photograph by Robert Ellsberg)

*"When the time came for me to take spiritual stock of myself, it was natural that I should do so by projecting my whole spiritual condition into the sphere of economic history and the class-struggle. In other words, the conclusion I came to was that it was not so much I myself that was to blame for my unhappiness, but the society in which I lived."*

(The Seven Storey Mountain)

ALMA MATER

ety. (His later religious conversion did not occasion a different attitude toward capitalism. "We live in a society," he reflected in *The Seven Storey Mountain*, "whose whole policy is to excite every nerve in the human body and keep it at the highest pitch of artificial tension, to strain every human desire to the limit and to create as many new desires and synthetic passions as possible, in order to cater to them with the products of our factories and printing presses and movie studios and all the rest."[72])

New York seemed better suited to revolutionary striving than London. Radical winds would certainly blow more easily at ritual-free Columbia University, "full of light and fresh air," than at tradition-bound Cambridge. Making his way to the concrete campus past piles of dirty snow, he signed up for modern language and literature courses that would in time result in a degree and open the way for him to find work as a journalist. During the summer he had tried to find work as a reporter, the editors who interviewed him told him to finish his university studies before reapplying.

In some ways Merton's life at Columbia wasn't altogether different than it had been at Cambridge. At parties he played the piano with wild enthusiasm, sang rowdy songs, drank his way into many hangovers, and seemed to find it a bragging point that he had fathered an illegitimate child in England.

But there were big differences. One was that he no longer lived in his own apartment, accountable only to himself, but was part of the Jenkins household, commuting to Manhattan from Long Island. Another contrast was in the classroom. Merton rejoiced in the informality that reigned between student and teacher in America.

The teacher who did the most to help Merton discover what was real in him was the poet Mark Van Doren, whose class in English literature Merton entered that first term, just after his twentieth birthday. Van Doren had a gift for posing the right questions. "You found yourself saying excellent things that you did not know you knew, and that you had not, in fact, known before. He had 'educed' them from you by his question. His classes were literally 'education'—they brought things out of you, they made your mind produce its own explicit ideas."[73] Van Doren didn't want to make his students into echoes of their teacher but to help them find the center within themselves. Neither was he swept along by current ideological fads, trimming Shakespeare to fit Marxist or Freudian patterns. As the first months passed, Merton was increasingly impressed that the "big sooty factory"[74] of Columbia University had on its faculty a man who was capable of teaching his students how to enter the heart of a book and how to tell a good book from a bad one.

It was partly because of people like Van Doren that Merton's enthusiasm for Communism dried up, though not all at once. Many Columbia students were Communists. They controlled the student newspaper and were a lively presence on campus. Merton joined a few picket lines, carrying posters

Above:
Mark Van Doren, professor of English Literature at Columbia, who impressed and influenced Merton. (Photograph courtesy of Columbia University)

*"Who is this man who does not have to fake and cover up a big gulf of ignorance by teaching a lot of opinions and conjectures and useless facts that belong to some other subject? Who is this that really loves what he has to teach, and does not secretly detest all literature, and abhor poetry, while pretending to be a professor of it? His classes were literally 'education'—they brought things out of you, they made your mind produce its own explicit ideas."*
(The Seven Storey Mountain)

with such messages as "Books, Not Battleships." During a student peace strike, he gave a speech on Communism in England, about which he knew practically nothing, but at least he still had the trace of an English accent. He sold some pamphlets and magazines. He attended a party in the Park Avenue apartment of a student whose wealthy parents were away for the weekend. "What a place for a machine-gun nest," said one of the aspiring revolutionaries.[75] That same evening Merton signed up as a member of the Young Communist League. In those days members got "Party names" in order to hide their real identity. Merton became Frank Swift. But he attended only one meeting of his cell group. There was a long discussion of why Comrade X had been missing meetings, the conclusion being that it was his father's fault. Merton left, walked into the fresh air of night, and let Frank Swift vanish in a glass of beer at a nearby bar. It was another act of joyful severance, "a sweet moment of silence and relief."[76]

Part of the problem with Communism for Merton was that it was only sporadically anti-war. The Communist Party was anti-war in 1935, the brief period when Merton was seriously attracted. The Party went pro-war during the Spanish Civil War in 1936, resumed an anti-war stance when Stalin signed the nonaggression pact with Hitler, then did another about-face when Hitler's armies attacked the Soviet Union. Merton, whose one radical action at Cambridge had been to sign a pacifist pledge, was not only looking for something with steadier principles but especially expected moral consistency about bloodshed. Merton came to realize that the Communist Party would "do whatever seems profitable to itself at the moment," which was, really, "the rule of all modern political parties."[77]

His only Marxist input that summer came from the Marx Brothers. John Paul, home from school in Pennsylvania, joined him in haunting movie theaters. Their cinematic partnership had begun the summer

"My active part in the world revolution was not very momentous. It lasted, in all, about three months . . . I decided that it would be wiser if I just remained a 'fellow-traveller.' The truth is that my inspiration to do something for the good of mankind had been pretty feeble and abstract from the start. I was still interested in doing good for only one person in the world—myself."

(The Seven Storey Mountain)

before. "I think John Paul and I and our various friends must have seen all the movies, without exception, that were produced from 1934 to 1937."[78] Tom's greatest heroes were Charlie Chaplin, W. C. Fields, and Harpo Marx. The only problem for the two brothers was that "we were almost always in danger of being thrown out of the theater for our uproarious laughter at scenes that were supposed to be most affecting, tender and appealing to the finer elements in the human soul—the tears of Jackie Cooper, the brave smile of Alice Faye behind the bars of a jail."[79]

Merton started classes in the fall of 1935 with a huge burst of energy, signing up for various courses (among them Spanish, German, geology, constitutional law, and contemporary civilization). He joined a fraternity, Alpha Delta Phi.

One of his fraternity brothers committed suicide that term, his body turning up in a canal two months later. On top of that, with his class in contemporary civilization, Merton visited the city morgue where he saw "rows and rows of iceboxes containing blue, swollen corpses" of those who had been fished out of the water or found on the streets, the murdered, the run-over, the suicides. It seemed to Merton that they were all casualties of contemporary civilization.[80]

Despite such harrowing glimpses of despair and death, it was all-systems-go in Merton's life. "I had ... a mysterious knack of keeping a hundred different interests going in the air at the same time."[81] At the heart of the juggling was his many hours spent in "the noisiest and most agitated part of the campus," the fourth floor of John Jay Hall. Here were the offices of several publications: *The Columbia Review*, *The Spectator*, *The Jester*, and the yearbook. Merton was there, writing stories and humorous columns, whenever he didn't have to be somewhere else. It was in these chaotic rooms that several of his life-long friendships had their genesis. Robert

Left:
Thomas Merton and Robert Lax in the editorial office of *Jester*, a Columbia student publication. (Photograph from the Columbia University Yearbook, courtesy of the Thomas Merton Studies Center)

*"The place [at Columbia] where I was busiest was the Jester office. Nobody really worked there, they just congregated about noontime and beat violently with the palms of their hands on the big empty filing cabinets, making a thunderous sound ... The chief advantage of [being editors of] Jester was that it paid most of our bills for tuition."*

(The Seven Storey Mountain)

Giroux, who later published *The Seven Storey Mountain*, was an editor of *The Review*, and Ed Rice, later Merton's godfather, was on *The Jester* staff. Both were Catholics.

Among the others working with *The Jester* was Bob Lax, as lean as an exclamation mark, a gentle prophet who seemed to be meditating on some impenetrable woe. This born contemplative could "curl his long legs all around a chair, in seven different ways, while he was trying to find the right word with which to begin." He possessed "a natural, instinctive spirituality, a kind of inborn direction to the living God." Lax saw Americans as longing to do good but not knowing how, waiting for the day when they could turn on the radio "and somebody will start telling them what they have really been wanting to hear and needing to know . . . somebody telling them of the love of God in language that will no longer sound hackneyed or crazy . . . "[82] At the end of the 1936 school year, Lax was elected editor of *The Jester* and Merton art editor.

Not only was work on *The Jester* staff a pleasure, but it paid most of Merton's tuition. Pocket money came from odd jobs, among them a stint working as guide and interpreter on the observation roof of the RCA building at Rockefeller Center, $27.50 a week, good money in 1936. He sold cartoons, $6 each, to a paper-cup manufacturer. As an occasional Latin tutor, he got $2.50 an hour. Paying his beer bill was no problem.

On top of everything else, there were all sorts of extracurricular activities: membership in the cross-country and track teams, the Laughing Lion Society, the Pre-Journalist Society (he was president for a time), the Philolexion (the school literary society), and various student committees.

The religious sparks that had been struck in Rome in 1933 flared again in October 1936 when Sam Jenkins died. "He had slipped out on us, in his sleep, without premeditation, on the spur of the

Left:
Merton on an outing with fraternity brothers. (Photograph from the Columbia University Yearbook, courtesy of the Thomas Merton Studies Center)

*"I suppose there were two reasons why I thought I ought to join a fraternity. One was the false one, that I thought it would help me to 'make connections' as the saying goes, and get a marvelous job on leaving college. The other, truer one was that I imagined that I would thus find a multitude of occasions for parties ... Both these hopes turned out to be illusory."*
(The Seven Storey Mountain)

moment."[83] Alone with the body in Douglaston, Merton felt he had to pray, and not just in his thoughts but on his knees. It was the sound of his grandmother's approaching steps that got him hurriedly back to his feet—still the old embarrassment about God. Martha Jenkins died the following August, Tom sitting at her side, praying silently as he listened to her struggle for breath.

Soon after her burial Merton had his own nightmarish scrape with death. On his way home by train to Douglaston one night, he seemed suddenly without balance. Feeling nauseated, he walked awkwardly to the passageway between cars, then nearly tumbled onto the tracks. Hanging on until he reached Pennsylvania Station, he checked into the hotel across the street and was given a room many floors above. A house doctor gave him some medicine and urged him to get some sleep. The floor seemed to tilt steeply toward the room's one window and the window to fill the wall. It was as if some murderous gravity were pulling him toward the window and to the air beyond, enticing him to submit. His head was spinning, but he clung onto life and in the morning walked out of the hotel through the front door.

A nervous breakdown brought on by another round of family deaths? Exhaustion from the heavy load at Columbia? The start of an ulcer, as the family doctor warned? Merton only knew that he had just barely survived and that no one was left of the family that raised him except John Paul and himself.

Left:
Thomas Merton in the Columbia quadrangle around 1939. (Photograph from the Columbia University Yearbook, courtesy of the Thomas Merton Studies Center)

*"Here I was, scarcely four years after I had left Oakham and walked out into the world I thought I was going to ransack and rob of all its pleasures and satisfactions. I had done what I intended, and now I found that it was I who was emptied and robbed and gutted."*
(The Seven Storey Mountain)

# Gilson, Huxley, Blake, and Maritain

*a world . . . charged with the presence and reality of God.*

Walking past Scribners Bookshop on Fifth Avenue in February 1937, Merton noticed *The Spirit of Medieval Philosophy* by Etienne Gilson. The title made him remember cloisters and cathedrals he had loved as a boy in the south of France: the authority, integrity, and grace of places of worship made by believing people living in an age of faith. He bought the book.

Opening it on the train ride home that day and glancing through the pages preceding the text, he found something more shocking than a refrigerated body in the city morgue: the Latin phrase *nihil obstat* ("without error") and the word, above a bishop's name, *imprimatur* ("let it be printed"): official certification that the book was consistent with Roman Catholic doctrine. For Merton the words meant the policing of the mind, the punishment of dissenters, and the enforcement of dogma.

"The feeling of disgust and deception struck me like a knife in the pit of my stomach," he recalled. "I felt as if I had been cheated! They should have warned me that it was a Catholic book! Then I would never have bought it. As it was, I was tempted to throw the thing out the window . . . to get rid of it as something dangerous and unclean."[84]

*"I had never had an adequate notion of what Christians meant by God."*
(The Seven Storey Mountain)

[45]

It was as if he had been given a thumbscrew used in the Inquisition. Merton could readily admire a cathedral building like Chartres and even appreciate some aspects of the life of prayer and worship it suggested, but not the religious structure that motivated the builders. He marveled at the culture of Catholicism but was horrified by the Catholic Church.

Merton's fascination with the subject matter took primacy over his loathing of censorship. He read the book straight through and from it became aware that orthodox Christian theology could be as profound and clean of line as any cathedral in France or Italy.

Gilson gave words to a nonverbal aesthetic sensitivity that had already marked Merton's religious development. Here was a theology with depth, spaciousness, and wholeness to match the icons that had moved him in Santa Sabina four years before.

He was especially moved by what Gilson wrote about God. Before Gilson, he admitted, "I had never had an adequate notion of what Christians meant by God. I had simply taken it for granted that the God in Whom religious people believed, and to Whom they attributed the creation and government of all things, was a noisy and dramatic and passionate character, a vague, jealous, hidden being."[85] The God in whom Catholics believed was not, as Merton previously imagined, an everlasting drill-sergeant, but rather, as Merton later put it, "mercy within mercy within mercy."[86] Merton put down Gilson's book with "an immense respect for Catholic philosophy and for the Catholic faith."[87]

That spring Merton started attending Sunday services at the Zion Church in Douglaston and had long talks about books with the church's pastor, Dr. Lester Riley. While enjoying their conversations, however, Merton found Riley's sermons lacked the theological substance that excited him in Gilson. "I wanted to hear about Doctrine, and nobody told me anything about Doctrine, about what to believe."[88]

In June Merton moved from Douglaston to a

Below:
Apartment on 114th St. where Merton lived after graduation from Columbia. (Photograph by Robert Ellsberg)

[46]

$7.50-a-week room on West 114th Street. It was here, at Bob Lax's urging, that he read Aldous Huxley's *Ends and Means*. The Huxley name, due to Aldous's biologist brother and scientist grandfather, was a synonym for religious skepticism. Yet here was a Huxley writing in defense of mysticism and urging his readers toward a life not only of prayer but asceticism.

Asceticism meant the art and discipline of living without society's normal comforts. "The very thought of such a thing was a complete revolution in my mind. The word had so far stood for a kind of weird and ugly perversion of nature, the masochism of men who had gone crazy in a warped and unjust society. What an idea! To deny the desires of one's flesh, and even to practice certain disciplines . . ."[89]

It occurred to Merton that, in failing to link ends and means within his life, the sorrows he had experienced were as inevitable as hangovers after too much beer. Huxley helped him realize that a purposeful detachment could be a way of opening oneself to a transforming encounter with God. The only thing that baffled Merton about Huxley was his preference for the Buddha over Christ. It was thanks to Huxley, however, that Merton took his first serious look at Buddhism, a subject he returned to later in life.

*Ends and Means* was also a pacifist book. Huxley agreed with Gandhi: people who forget about means become mean people, and murderous methods create murderous societies; while prayer and asceticism are the foundation of spiritual life, a nonviolent life is the only possible way to create a nonviolent society.

With the Spanish Civil War underway, nonviolence was far from popular among students at Columbia. Those to the right sided with Franco, those to the left with Spain's radical Republicans. The only point of agreement on both sides was the necessity of bloodshed. Among those who died on the Republican side in 1937 was a Columbia alumnus.

*"[Huxley] showed that this negation [asceticism] was not something absolute, sought for its own sake: but that it was a freeing, a vindication of our real selves, a liberation of the spirit from limits and bonds that were intolerable, suicidal—from a servitude to flesh that must ultimately destroy our whole nature and society and the world as well."*

(The Seven Storey Mountain)

Having received his bachelor of arts diploma in February 1938, Merton entered Columbia's Graduate School of English where he chose to write his thesis on one of the great dissenters of the eighteenth century, the poet and mystic William Blake.

Blake stood in opposition to those who saw nothing more in the mystery of life than the puzzles of chemistry and who regarded mysticism as madness. With the searing conviction of a biblical prophet, Blake rejoiced that

> The atoms of Democritus
> And Newton's particles of light
> Are sands upon the Red-Sea Shore
> Where Israel's tents do shine so bright.[90]

The more he read Blake, the more impressed Merton was with the poet's unwillingness to adjust himself to an age that was simultaneously pious, grasping, self-satisfied, and indifferent to the poor. He was captivated by Blake's poetry. "He wrote better poetry when he was twelve than Shelley wrote in his whole life. And it was because, at twelve, he had already seen, I think, Elias standing under a tree in the fields south of London."[91]

Blake represented a quality of mind that neither gazed at the world through the rose-tinted glasses of romanticism nor, in the name of reason, looked at creation with eyes dead to God's presence and activity. The Blake who had seen Elias under a tree also saw British fortunes being minted in "dark Satanic mills"[92] owned by pitiless men who went to church on Sunday. "Blake saw," Merton wrote, "that, in the legislation of men, some evils had been set up as standards of right by which other evils were to be condemned: and the norms of pride or greed had been established in the judgment seat, to pronounce a crushing and inhuman indictment against all the normal healthy strivings of human nature. Love was outlawed, and became lust, pity was swallowed up in

Above:
Head of Job. (Drawing by William Blake)

*"[Blake's] rebellion, for all its strange heterodoxy, was fundamentally the rebellion of the saints. It was the rebellion of the lover of the living God, the rebellion of one whose desire of God was so intense and irresistible that it condemned, with all its might, all the hypocrisy and petty sensuality and skepticism and materialism which cold and trivial minds set up as unpassable barriers."*

(The Seven Storey Mountain)

[48]

cruelty, and so Blake knew how 'The harlot's cry from street to street/Shall weave old England's winding sheet.' "[93]

"What a thing it was," Merton recalled, "to live in contact with the genius and holiness of William Blake that year. . . . By the time the summer was over, I was to become conscious of the fact that the only way to live was to live in a world that was charged with the presence and reality of God."[94]

That same year a mild Hindu monk appeared in Merton's life. Bramachari had been sent from his ashram in India to take part in a Congress of Religions at the World's Fair in Chicago but had arrived too late. He stayed on in America, living from whatever contributions and kindnesses came his way. He was in New York thanks to Merton's friends, Sy and Helen Freedgood, living quietly in their home despite a grandmother who worried that this Asian in turban, white robes, and tattered sneakers might be an enemy of the Jewish people. Merton had been part of the welcoming committee when Bramachari arrived from Chicago and in subsequent weeks spent long hours talking with him.

"He was never sarcastic, never ironical or unkind in his criticisms: in fact he did not make many judgments at all, especially adverse ones," Merton wrote a decade later. "He would simply make statements of fact, and then burst out laughing—his laughter was quiet and ingenuous, and it expressed his complete amazement at the very possibility that people should live the way he saw them living all around him."[95]

Americans often asked Bramachari about the progress of Christian missionaries in India. Bramachari's response impressed Merton. The problem was, he said, that they lived too comfortably, "in a way that simply made it impossible for Hindus to regard them as holy—let alone the fact that they ate meat." Hindus were amazed that Christians weren't ascetics.[96]

For all his friendly criticisms of meat-eating missionaries, Bramachari played a Christian missionary role in Merton's life. "He did not generally put his words in the form of advice, but the one counsel he did give me is something that I will not easily forget: 'There are many beautiful mystical books written by the Christians. You should read Saint Augustine's *Confessions*, and *The Imitation of Christ*. . . . Yes, you must read those books' "[97] In his room on 114th Street Merton started reading *The Imitation of Christ* and started praying again, "more or less regularly."[98]

Summer heat drove Merton up to a place Lax had in Olean, a quiet town in western New York State, but in a week Merton was back in Manhattan "on account of being, as usual, in love."[99]

In September, while busy with his thesis, "Nature and Art in William Blake,"[100] he found time to read another book that sharpened his attraction to Catholicism, Jacques Maritain's *Art and Scholasticism*. If Gilson had helped give Merton back the word *God*, Maritain resurrected the word *virtue*. He used the term without embarrassment, secure in the word's Latin meaning — strength. Merton came away from Maritain's book with a "sane conception of virtue — without which there can be no happiness, because virtues are precisely the powers by which we come to acquire happiness."[101]

*"By the time the summer was over, I was to become conscious of the fact that the only way to live was to live in a world that was charged with the presence and reality of God."*
(The Seven Storey Mountain)

# Conversion

*Even the ugly buildings of Columbia were transfigured.*

One weekend in August 1938 it struck Merton that he had "been in and out of a thousand Catholic cathedrals and churches, and yet I had never heard Mass." On those occasions when he happened to find the liturgy was being celebrated, he fled "in wild Protestant panic." Now he began to feel "a sweet, strong, gentle, clean urge in me which said: 'Go to Mass! Go to Mass!' "[102]

Canceling a weekend date in the country with the woman he had been dating, he had, as it seemed to him, his first sober Sunday in New York since leaving England. It was a dazzling day of blue skies and vacant avenues.

The church he walked to was Corpus Christi, just behind Columbia Teachers College on West 121st Street. Wanting to watch but not be noticed, he found an obscure spot inside.

"The first thing I noticed was a young girl, very pretty too, perhaps fifteen or sixteen, kneeling straight up and praying quite seriously. I was very much impressed to see that someone who was young and beautiful could with such simplicity make prayer the real and serious and principal reason for going to church."[103] Looking around, he realized her attitude was quite typical. These were people who didn't seem to take any notice of themselves. They were matter-of-factly on their knees, all attention focused on the altar.

Below:
Plaque outside Corpus Christi Church on West 121st St. (Photograph by Robert Ellsberg)

*"How bright the little building seemed. Indeed, it was quite new. The sun shone on the clean bricks. People were going in that wide open door, into the cool darkness and, all at once, all the churches of Italy and France came back to me. The richness and fullness of the atmosphere of Catholicism that I had not been able to avoid apprehending and loving as a child, came back to me with a rush . . . "*
(The Seven Storey Mountain)

[51]

Afterward, walking in the sun along Broadway, Merton felt that he was in a new world. "I could not understand what it was that had happened to make me so happy, why I was so much at peace, so content with life. . . . Even the ugly buildings of Columbia were transfigured."[104] Eating breakfast at Childs on 111th Street, a place that usually struck him as gloomy and small, he felt as if he were in the Elysian Fields.

If intellectually he was moving with saints and mystics, even overcoming his last inhibitions about Catholicism, day-to-day life in many ways was still much the same. On Labor Day he drove with a friend to Philadelphia, stopping on the way at "a big dark roadhouse, arguing and arguing about mysticism, and smoking more and more cigarettes and gradually getting drunk."[105] It took days to recover from the hangover.

Yet the next Sunday he was back at Mass, and the next and the next. During those weeks it was enough just to stand by and admire the sacramental life others were leading.

In contrast to his quiet romance with Catholicism, grim events were occurring on the other side of the Atlantic: The Spanish Civil War was nearing its end, adding Spain to the list of fascist regimes in Europe, while Hitler's Germany was expanding to the east. The Nazis who had run Merton off the road in 1933 were now running whole nations off the road. While Neville Chamberlain was talking about "peace in our time" on his return from Munich at the end of September, it seemed to Merton that a general holocaust was much more likely.

"I was very depressed," he wrote. "I was beyond thinking about the intricate and filthy political tangle that underlay the mess. I had given up politics as more or less hopeless, by this time. I was no longer interested in having any opinion about the movement and interplay of forces that were all more or less iniquitous and corrupt, and it was far too laborious and uncertain a business to try and find out some degree of truth and justice in all the loud, artificial claims that were put forward by the various sides. ... The future was obscured, blanked out by war as by a dead-end wall. Nobody knew if anybody at all would come out of it alive. Who would be worse off, the civilians or the soldiers? The distinction between their fates was to be abolished ... by aerial warfare."

All the internal contradictions of the society in which Merton lived were converging within him. He could see that "my likes or dislikes, beliefs or disbeliefs meant absolutely nothing in the external, political order. I was just an individual, and the individual had ceased to count. ... I would probably soon become a number on the list of those to be drafted. I would get a piece of metal with my number on it ... so as to help out the circulation of red-tape that would necessarily follow the disposal of my remains."[106]

It was in the midst of such dark thoughts that another important book landed in Merton's life, G. F. Leahy's biography of English poet and Jesuit priest Gerard Manley Hopkins.

Sitting in his room on West 114th Street on a wet fall day, Merton started reading a chapter that described Hopkins's conversion to Catholicism while a student at Oxford in 1866.

"All of a sudden," Merton recalled in his autobiography, "something began to stir within me, something began to push me, to prompt me. It was a movement that spoke like a voice. 'What are you waiting for?' it said. 'Why are you sitting here? Why do you still hesitate? You know what you ought to do? Why don't you do it?'

"I stirred in the chair. I lit a cigarette, looked out the window at the rain, tried to shut the voice up. 'Don't act on your impulses,' I thought. 'This is crazy. This is not rational. Read your book.' "

He tried to press on with Hopkins's life, but the

Below:
Gerard Manley Hopkins, the English poet and convert who became a Jesuit priest.

inner voice only renewed its appeal: "It's useless to hesitate any longer. Why don't you get up and go?" He read another few sentences about Hopkins's conversion, and then came his own moment of consent. "I could bear it no longer. I put down the book, and got into my raincoat, and started down the stairs. I went out into the street. I crossed over, and walked along by the grey wooden fence, towards Broadway, in the light rain. And then everything inside me began to sing."[107]

Nine blocks away was Corpus Christi and its presbytery, to which Father Ford, the pastor, was just returning.

Left:
Corpus Christi Church, where Merton was baptized. (Photograph by Robert Ellsberg)

*"It was a gay, clean church, with big plain windows and white columns and pilasters and a well-lighted, simple sanctuary. Its style was a trifle eclectic, but much less perverted with incongruities than the average Catholic church in America. It had a kind of a seventeenth-century, oratorian character about it, though with a sort of American colonial tinge of simplicity."*
(The Seven Storey Mountain)

"Father," Merton asked, "may I speak to you about something?"

"Yes, sure, come into the house."

They sat in the parlor.

"Father, I want to become a Catholic."[108]

Father Ford gave him three books to read and arranged for Merton to return for instruction two evenings a week.

The news of his impending baptism was broken to Bob Lax with a frisbee-like toss of his hat. "I remember the moment," said Lax, "because he'd never before, and never since, thrown a hat in my direction."[109] On November 18 Merton was baptized.

"What do you ask from God's Church?" Merton was asked. "Faith!" "What does faith bring you?" "Life everlasting."

Witnessing the rite of passage were four friends, three of them Jews: Bob Lax, Sy Freedgood, and Bob Gerdy; only his godfather, Ed Rice, was Catholic.

Merton entered a confessional for the first time, worried that the young priest sitting on the other side of the partition might be shocked to hear some of the events and habits that were about to be recounted. "But one by one, species by species, as best I could, I tore out all those sins by their roots, like teeth. Some of them were hard." Baptized and absolved, for the first time he was not only present at Mass but was able to receive communion. "Now I had entered into the everlasting movement of that gravitation which is the very life and spirit of God ... goodness without end. ... He called out to me from His own immense depths."[110]

# Brother John Merton, OFM

*We all had a sort of feeling that we could be hermits up on the hill.*

Having been awarded his master's degree in February 1939, Merton started work on a doctoral dissertation about Gerard Manley Hopkins. He moved to a one-room apartment with wrought-iron balcony at 35 Perry Street in Greenwich Village, Manhattan's literary heartland.

His religious life was steadily deepening. He was at Mass every Sunday, often on weekdays, and occasionally stopped in church to pray, make the stations of the cross, or recite the rosary. Conversion had brought him that far. But preparing for confession on alternate Saturdays, it seemed to him his life still had the smell of beer and cigarettes. What conversion should mean in terms of his future life and work was still hidden.

The obvious choices were writing and teaching. His education had prepared him for the classroom; he knew from Mark Van Doren, now a friend, what role a teacher could play in a student's life. Writing seemed inescapable; he would be a writer if for no other reason than he was incapable of not writing. When not busy with academic projects, he was at work on a novel. He was writing poetry as well. His baptism seemed to have brought with it "a sudden facility for rough, raw Skeltonic verses."[111] Rejection slips were arriving from some of the best magazines in the country. "How many envelopes I fed to the green mailbox at the corner of Perry Street just

Opposite:
Shrine of Our Lady of Cobre in Cuba, where Merton made a retreat in the spring of 1940. (Photograph by Elaine Williams, courtesy of Maryknoll archives)

Below:
Merton's apartment on Perry Street in Greenwich Village. (Photograph by Robert Ellsberg)

before you got to Seventh Avenue! And everything I put in there came back—except for the book reviews."[112]

He was dating a nurse but was in no hurry to get married. He was quietly wrestling with the idea of ordination to the priesthood and thus a life of celibacy, a word that both fascinated him and gave him the cold sweats. But he worried that, as a priest, he would no longer be able to write the way he wanted to. The word *imprimatur* was never to become a comforting sound in his ear.

For Lax, the question wasn't so much *what* to become as *who* to become. Lax, though not yet Catholic himself, had steadily encouraged Merton in his religious search. It was Lax more than anyone who challenged Merton to aim high in the life of grace and not allow joining the church to be the high-water mark of his religious development.

Walking on Sixth Avenue one night in the spring of 1939, Lax turned toward Merton and asked, "What do you want to be, anyway?"

It was obvious to Merton that "Thomas Merton the well-known writer" and "Thomas Merton the assistant instructor of Freshman English" were not good enough answers.

"I don't know," he finally said. "I guess what I want is to be a good Catholic."

"What do you mean, you want to be a good Catholic?"

Merton was silent. He hadn't figured that out yet.

"What you should say," Lax went on, "is that you want to be a saint."

That struck Merton as downright weird.

"How do you expect me to become a saint?"

"By wanting to."

"I can't be a saint," Merton responded. To be a saint would require a magnitude of renunciation that was completely beyond him. But Lax pressed on.

"All that is necessary to be a saint is to want to be one. Don't you believe God will make you what

Above:
Robert Lax. (Photograph courtesy of Boston College, Burns Library)

*Bob Lax was a potential prophet, but without rage. A king, but a Jew too. A mind full of tremendous and subtle intuitions, and every day he found less and less to say about them, and resigned himself to being inarticulate. In his hesitations, though without embarrassment or nervousness at all, he would often curl his long legs all around a chair in seven different ways, while he was trying to find a word with which to begin. . . . Lax has always been afraid he was in a blind alley, and half aware that, after all, it might not be a blind alley, but God, infinity."*
(The Seven Storey Mountain)

He created you to be, if you will consent to let Him do it? All you have to do is desire it."[113]

Giving himself time to think about what sanctity might mean in his case, Merton sublet the Perry Street apartment and went off with Lax and Ed Rice to spend the summer in a one-room cottage near Olean where the three of them set up their typewriters and proceeded to write novels, pausing occasionally for hamburgers, beans, milk, and bongo-playing. Rice's book was called *The Blue Horse*; Lax worked on *The Spangled Palace*; and Merton struggled with a book that started out as *The Straights of Dover*, became *The Night before the Battle*, and was finally christened *The Labyrinth*. The writing was fun and being on the top of a wooded mountain listening to birds and wind wasn't the worst thing that could happen during the weeks when Manhattan was sweating out the heat. "We all had a sort of feeling that we could be hermits up on the hill," Merton recalled, "but the trouble was that none of us really knew how and I, who was in a way the most articulate, as well as the least sensible whenever it came to matters of conduct and discussions concerning good and evil, still had the strongest urges to go down into the valleys and see what was on at the movies, or play the slot machines, or drink beer."[114]

Back in New York, Merton began to send his manuscript around and to pray fervently that some publisher would like it, but it attracted only rejection letters. "Other people's bad books get published," he noted in his journal. "Why can't my bad book get published?"

Meanwhile the situation in Europe was becoming more disastrous by the day, the Nazis confident that they were in the early stages of their thousand-year reign. As he pondered the headlines, it occurred to Merton that a Christian couldn't simply blame others or accuse history for the Nazi nightmare: "I myself am responsible for this," he realized. "My sins

*"I made the terrible mistake of entering upon the Christian life as if it were merely the natural life invested with a kind of supernatural mode by grace. I thought that all I had to do was to continue living as I had lived before, thinking and acting as I did before, with the one exception of avoiding mortal sin."*
(The Seven Storey Mountain)

have done this. Hitler is not the only one who has started this war: I have my share in it too."[115] On the first day of World War II, with bombs falling on Warsaw, Merton received communion in the Church of Saint Francis of Assisi, near Pennsylvania Station, aware that the same Christ he was receiving was "being nailed again to the cross by the effect of my sins, and the sins of the whole, selfish, stupid, idiotic world of men."[116]

Days were given to his typewriter, nights to friends, movies, beer, jazz, boogie-woogie and dancing. Merton wasn't only a listener but a player when it came to jazz. Jinny Burton, the woman he was dating most frequently, wondered if he wouldn't be happier as a jazz pianist rather than a novelist.

It was after an intense night at a jazz club and a crowd of friends sleeping over in his apartment on Perry Street that Merton, struggling with a hangover, experienced a wave of disgust at the life he was leading and turned with fresh intensity to the idea of becoming a priest. At a nearby Catholic library he borrowed a small book about the Jesuits. Reading it until it was dark outside, he went to the Jesuit Church of Saint Francis Xavier on 16th Street. A service of adoration of the Blessed Sacrament was going on. He knelt, fixing his eyes on the white host in its gold monstrance on the altar, and listened once again to the questioning voice inside himself, "Do you really want to be a priest? If you do, say so." As the priest raised the monstrance and blessed the people, "I looked straight at the Host, and I knew, now, Who it was that I was looking at, and I said: 'Yes, I want to be a priest, with all my heart I want it. If it is Your will, make me a priest.' "[117]

One of the most helpful voices in Merton's life at this crucial moment belonged to Dan Walsh. Walsh taught a class on Saint Thomas Aquinas for which Merton signed up. A small, stocky man who looked like a friendly prize fighter, Walsh taught with

Above:
Church of St. Francis of Assisi on 31st St., where Merton often prayed. (Photograph by Robert Ellsberg)

[60]

"childlike delight and cherubic simplicity," helping his students understand the spirit and theological structure of Catholicism. He had, said Merton, "the most rare and admirable virtue of being able to rise above the petty differences of schools and systems [as represented by such theologians as Augustine, Aquinas, Bonaventure, and Duns Scotus], seeing Catholic philosophy in its wholeness."[118] Walsh knew Etienne Gilson, whose book Merton had nearly thrown out the train window on discovering its *imprimatur*, and Jacques Maritain.

It was to Walsh that Merton first mentioned the possibility of becoming a priest. The two were walking together on Park Avenue. "Dan turned to me and said, 'You know, the first time I met you I thought you had a vocation to the priesthood.'"[119]

Walsh surveyed the variety of religious orders within the Catholic Church, the Benedictines, Dominicans, Franciscans, Jesuits, and others. Not least in Walsh's estimation were the Trappists. Walsh had recently spent a week at a Trappist monastery in Kentucky, the Abbey of Our Lady of Gethsemani, and spoke with excitement of the Trappists' penitential way of life: hours in church each day, silence except in prayer, hard physical labor on the abbey's farmland, rigorous fasts.

Walsh asked Merton, "Do you think you would like that kind of life?"

"Oh no," Merton said with alarm, "not a chance! That's not for me! I'd never be able to stand it. It would kill me in a week." He pictured a vast gray prison with dour inmates, hoods pulled down over their faces. The Trappists' official name — the Order of Cistercians of the Strict Observance — made Merton shiver.

"Well," Walsh replied, "it's a good thing you know yourself so well."[120]

The Jesuits appealed to Merton. Gerard Manley Hopkins had been a Jesuit. Among Jesuits writing was a cherished vocation. But the Franciscans

Below:
Church of St. Francis Xavier on W. 16th St. (Photograph by Robert Ellsberg)

*"Do you really want to be a priest? If you do, say so . . . I looked straight at the Host and I knew, now, Who it was that I was looking at, and I said: 'Yes, I want to be a priest, with all my heart I want it. If it is Your will, make me a priest.'"*

(The Seven Storey Mountain)

seemed the order best suited to his temperament. Francis of Assisi had lived a life of literal acceptance of the teachings of Jesus, joyfully renouncing power, refusing property, and prohibiting all violence. While the Franciscan movement had been institutionalized after the founder's death, it remained welcoming, cheerful, active in the world—nothing like the prison-style monasticism Merton imagined was typical of the Trappists.

With a letter of recommendation from Dan Walsh in hand, Merton went to talk with Father Edmund at the Franciscan monastery on 31st Street. Their discussions went well, Merton's only disappointment being that he would have to wait ten months, until August 1940, when the next novitiate group was formed. So eager was he to turn the page, the delay seemed like an eternity to Merton. While waiting out the year, Father Edmund urged Merton to accept a job teaching at Columbia while continuing work on his doctorate.

At the urging of a Franciscan he talked to in confession, Merton started going to Mass and communion on a daily basis. He felt his life was being transformed. Friends remarked how happy he seemed.

While teaching an English composition course at Columbia he continued writing, sending out submissions, and receiving rejection slips. In the process he found an agent, Naomi Burton, who liked *The Labyrinth* and was willing to help him with his future work. She became not only his agent and friendly critic but a friend for life.

In April 1940, Merton went on an Easter trip to Cuba, a journey that was part pilgrimage to the shrine of Our Lady of Cobre, part vacation.[121] Both elements were experienced with intensity. Even when walking in parts of Havana that were anything but pilgrimage places, he felt wrapped in a kind of innocence and simplicity he had never known in adult life.

Above:
Daniel Walsh, a professor of philosophy at Columbia, was the one to whom Merton turned for advice about his religious vocation. (Photograph courtesy of Columbia University)

"[P]erhaps the impression that [Dan Walsh] made was all the more forceful because his square jaw had a kind of potential toughness about it. Yet . . . there he sat, this little, stocky man who had something of the appearance of a good-natured prize fighter, smiling and talking with the most childlike delight and cherubic simplicity about the Summa Theologica."
(The Seven Storey Mountain)

During the consecration at Mass in the Church of Saint Francis in Havana, among crowds of school children, Merton had a stunning experience of the divine presence:

The bell rang again, three times. Before any head was raised the clear cry of the brother in the brown robe cut through the silence with the words "Yo creo ... " [I believe] which immediately all the children took up after him with such loud and strong and clear voices, and such unanimity and such meaning and such fervor that something went off inside me like a thunderclap and without seeing anything or apprehending anything extraordinary through any of my senses (my eyes were open on only precisely what was there, the church), I knew with the most absolute and unquestion-able certainty that before me, between me and the altar, somewhere in the center of the church, up in the air (or any other place because in no place), but directly before my eyes, or directly present to some apprehension or other of mine which was above that of the senses, was at the same time God in all His essence, all His power, all His glory, and God in Himself and God surrounded by the radiant faces of the uncountable thousands upon thousands of saints contemplating His glory and praising His Holy Name. And so the unshakable certainty, the clear and immediate knowledge that Heaven was right in front of me, struck me like a thunderbolt and went through me like a flash of lightning and seemed to lift me clean up off the earth.[122]

> *The white girls open their arms like clouds,*
> *The black girls close their eyes like wings:*
> *Angels bow down like bells,*
> *Angels look up like toys,*
>
> *Because the heavenly stars*
> *Stand in a ring:*
> *And all the pieces of the mosaic, earth,*
> *Get up and fly away like birds.*
> ("Song for Our Lady of Cobre")

In *The Seven Storey Mountain,* Merton again sought to describe what he had experienced:

It was a light that was so bright that it had no relation to any visible light and so profound and so intimate that it seemed like a neutralization of every lesser experience. And yet the thing that struck me most of all was that this light was in a certain sense "ordinary"—it was a light (and this most of all was what took my breath away) that was offered to all, to everybody, and there was nothing fancy or strange about it. . . . It disarmed all images, all metaphors. . . . It ignored all sense experience in order to strike directly at the heart of truth . . . it . . . belonged to the order of knowledge, yes, but more still to the order of love.[123]

While at the shrine of Our Lady of Cobre, Merton made a promise to Mary that, should he ever be ordained a priest, he would offer his vocation to her.

Back in New York in June, Merton received the news that certain essential papers, such as the marriage certificate of his parents, had been received and his application to enter the Franciscan novitiate had been accepted.

Summer began with a trip to Ithaca to visit John Paul, then a student at Cornell. John Paul seemed quite lost, reminding Merton of himself in Cambridge. John Paul was fascinated by the change occurring in Tom's life. The Christmas before he had given Tom a rosary as a token of support. While they were together in Ithaca, he went with his brother to Mass, not just watching but kneeling at his side.

The next stop was Olean where Merton, Lax, and Rice were once again going to work on novels, this time joined by Bob Gibney and Sy Freedgood. Merton made arrangements to bunk at the nearby Franciscan college, St. Bonaventure's, using a dilapidated room in the gymnasium. This put him close to the monastery chapel where he received communion every morning. Most of the others present were young Franciscan novices. He pictured himself in brown robe and leather sandals bearing the name Brother John.

Below:
The Franciscan monastery on W. 31st St., where Merton applied for admission to the order. (Photograph by Robert Ellsberg)

The previous summer conversation in the writers' cottage on the hill had practically nothing to do with the events in Europe. In the summer of 1940 it was one of their chief topics. Belgium, Holland, and much of France were occupied by the German army. Rotterdam had been gutted, the first city to be destroyed in the war. "We sat around the fireplace at night and talked about the Selective Service Law that would soon be passed in Washington, wondering how it would be and what we should do about it."[124] Lax was wondering whether this war or any war was justified. Gibney wasn't quite pacifist but felt, even if he went into the army, he could not bear arms, a position similar to Merton's, though the issue seemed less personal to him as members of religious communities, as he would be soon, were exempt from the draft.

But as the summer progressed, Merton began to have doubts about his Franciscan vocation. These were due in part to a vague disappointment with Franciscan life, which had begun to strike him as too tame. What troubled him most, however, was that he had given Dan Walsh and Father Edmund a streamlined version of his life story. Major pieces had been left out, most of all the fact that he had fathered a child in England. The Franciscans, he concluded, simply accepted him because he was superficially presentable, a young man with a sincere face, not the real Tom Merton but a cardboard cut-out. As he thought it over, "it began to appear utterly impossible that anyone in his right mind could consider me fit material for the priesthood."[125]

Back in New York, he went to see Father Edmund and filled in the blank spaces. Father Edmund told Merton he needed a day to think over what he had been told. The next day he asked Merton to withdraw his application.

"It seemed to me," Merton wrote, "that I was now excluded from the priesthood forever." He walked in a daze to a church on Seventh Avenue,

Above:
Church of Our Lady of Guadalupe on 14th St. (Photograph by Robert Ellsberg)

*"So I knelt at the altar rail in the little Mexican church of Our Lady of Guadalupe . . . where I sometimes went to Communion, and asked with great intensity of desire for the publication of the book, if it should be for God's glory. The fact that I could even calmly assume that there was some possibility of the book giving glory to God shows the profound depths of my ignorance and spiritual blindness: but anyway, that was what I asked."*

(The Seven Storey Mountain)

[65]

went into a confessional, tried to tell the priest what had happened, and began to cry uncontrollably. The priest told Merton no one like him belonged in any monastery, still less in the priesthood. "He gave me to understand that I was simply wasting his time."[126] Feeling utterly abandoned, Merton wept in one of the pews until the tears were running down the fingers in which he hid his face.

Though the doors to religious community and a priestly vocation had been closed, Merton realized he could lead a more committed religious life, however privately. In addition to continuing his participation in daily Mass, he bought a four-volume breviary and cleared patches of time during the day to recite the monastic prayer offices.

*"I had to be led by a way that I could not understand, and I had to follow a path that was beyond my own choosing."*
(The Seven Storey Mountain)

"I did not have any lofty theories about the vocation of the lay-contemplative," he recalled in his autobiography. "In fact, I no longer dignified what I was trying to do by the name of a vocation. All I knew was that I wanted grace, and that I needed prayer, and that I was helpless without God, and that I wanted to do everything that people did to keep close to Him. . . . All that occupied me now was the immediate practical problem of getting up my hill with this terrific burden I had on my shoulders, step by step, begging God to drag me along."[127]

# St. Bonaventure's

*Destruction is all I remember.*

In the fall of 1940 Merton took a job teaching English at St. Bonaventure's College in Olean. The friars paid him $45 a month plus room and board. He tacked up several images on the door of his room: Saint Francis receiving the stigmata, Saint Dominic the missionary preacher, two of Mary and Jesus, an Annunciation by Dürer.

"I had three big classes of sophomores, ninety students, ninety students in all, to bring through English Literature from Beowulf to the Romantic Revival in one year. And a lot of them didn't know how to spell. But that didn't even worry me very much, and it could not alter my happiness with *Piers Plowman* and *The Nun's Priest's Tale.* . . . I was back again in that atmosphere that had enthralled me as a child, the serene and simple and humorous Middle Ages . . . the twelfth and thirteenth and fourteenth centuries, full of fresh air and simplicity, as solid as wheat bread and grape wine and water-mills and ox-drawn wagons: the age of Cistercian monasteries and the first Franciscans."[128]

His students ranged from athletes to seminarians. He was surprised how much he enjoyed teaching football players. They "were the best-natured and the best-tempered and worked as hard as the seminarians. They were also the most vocal. They liked to talk about these books when I stirred them up to argue. . . . [They] taught me much more about people than I taught them about books." The seminari-

Below:
Merton at St. Bonaventure. (Photograph by F. Donald Kenney, courtesy of St. Bonaventure University)

*"It amazed me how swiftly my life fell into a plan of fruitful and pleasant organization here under the roof with these Friars, in this house dedicated to God."*
(The Seven Storey Mountain)

ans were quieter. "They kept pretty much to themselves, and handed in neat papers." Whatever the students' temperaments and ambitions in life, it was alarming to Merton that they all seemed to share the view "that the modern world was the highest point reached by man in his development, and that our present civilization left very little to be desired."[129]

For Merton, the age of Saint Francis ranked higher. While at St. Bonaventure's he joined the Franciscan movement for lay associates, the Third Order. Members wore a scapular under their clothes — a chord with two small pieces of brown material similar to the fabric used in Franciscan robes. For Merton this served as a symbol that he was a monk of some kind even if without formal membership in a religious community. He tried to make headway in his religious life not only on his knees but at the table. He cut back on meat, but felt guilty he couldn't give it up completely. He fought with his long-running addiction to movies, doing about as well with this as with meat.

Not all his shortcomings were minor. He tried to live a celibate life but failed. The event is only hinted at in his autobiography: "If I had ever thought I had become immune from passion, and that I did not have to fight for freedom, there was no chance of that illusion any more."[130]

Merton was haunted by the expanding war in Europe. Always one to notice strands of connection between pastures and battlefields, he wrote in his diary: "The valley is full of oil storage tanks, and oil is for feeding bombers, and once they are fed they have to bomb something, and they generally pick on oil tanks. Wherever you have oil tanks, or factories, or railroads or any of the comforts of home and manifestations of progress, in this century, you are sure to get bombers, sooner or later. Therefore, if I don't pretend . . . to understand the war, I do know this much: that the knowledge of what is going on only makes it seem desperately important to be voluntarily poor, to get rid of all possessions this instant."[131]

He may have been influenced by Saint Francis, who once explained to his bishop why the members of his community couldn't own property: "If we held property, armed force for protection would become necessary. For property gives rise to lawsuits and to wars which in various ways destroy all love of God and of our fellowmen. Our membership, therefore, will not hold property."

Merton's thoughts about the war found their main expression in a novel he wrote while teaching at St. Bonaventure's, *The Journal of My Escape from the Nazis* (published in 1969 as *My Argument with the Gestapo*). The story followed a poet's return to war-ravaged London from America. Though coming from America, the narrator, Merton in every detail but name, is a stateless person. "I have lived in too many countries," he explains, "to have a nationality."[132]

Why do you come back? he is asked. "Not to fight," he says. He admits he has come to write. What will you write? "I will say that . . . the things I remember are destroyed, but that does not mean as much as it seems, because the destruction was already going on before, and destruction is all I remember."[133]

Later the question is posed: But isn't the war Germany's fault? "In the sense that they began fighting it, yes." Doesn't that mean Germany is guilty? "I don't know the meaning of the word guilty, except in the sense that I am also guilty for the war, partly." But it is nations that are guilty of war. "Nations don't exist. They can't be held responsible for anything. Nations are made up of people, and people are responsible for the things they do." In that case, Hitler is the guilty one. "He might be. Only I don't know enough about it. He might be more guilty than any other one person, but he isn't the only person guilty of the war. . . . All I know is, if anything happens to the world, it is partly because of me."[134]

The narrator explains to an officer who is interrogating him, "You think you can identify a man by giving his date of birth and his address, his height, his

Left:
Bombing of London, the tower of St. Paul's Cathedral in the background. (Photograph courtesy of Maryknoll archives)

*"Morning after morning when I glanced at the New York Times in the library, between classes, I read the headlines about the cities that had been cut to pieces with bombs. Night after night the huge dark mass of London was bursting into wide areas of flame that turned its buildings into empty craters and cariated those miles and miles of slums. Around St. Paul's the ancient City was devastated . . . "*

(The Seven Storey Mountain)

eyes' color, even his fingerprints. Such information will help you put the right tag on his body if you should run across his body somewhere full of bullets, but it doesn't say anything about the man himself. Men become objects and not persons. Now you complain because there is a war, but war is the proper state for a world in which men are a series of numbered bodies. War is the state that now perfectly fits your philosophy of life: you deserve the war for believing the things you believe. In so far as I tend to believe those same things and act according to such lies, I am part of the complex of responsibilities for the war too. But if you want to identify me, ask me not where I live, or what I like to eat, or how I comb my hair, but ask me what I think I am living for, in detail, and ask me what I think is keeping me from living fully for the thing I want to live for."[135]

It was an autobiographical novel written by a man using his typewriter as a confessional, confessing not only specific sins he has committed but his co-responsibility for sins that are destroying the world.

The novel was also a confession of what he would do personally in the war: he would not kill anyone. He found no invitation to killing in the words and life of Jesus, who had lived an unarmed and healing life under the tyranny of Roman occupation. In the thirteenth century Saint Francis had renewed the nonviolent witness of the early church, writing a pacifist rule not only for his friars and nuns but for lay people too. His rule for the Third Order had forbidden members to possess weapons or use them for any reason.

When Merton registered with the Selective Service, it was as a conscientious objector, though prepared for noncombatant service on the battlefield as an unarmed medic. In such a role, he wrote in his journal, "I would not have to kill men made in the image and likeness of God" but could obey the divine law of "serving the wounded and saving lives." Even if it turned out that he would only dig latrines, he considered this "a far greater honor to God than killing men."[136]

Writing his autobiography fifteen years later, he expanded on his decision in a text which startled many readers, appearing as it did in the early days of the Cold War:

[God] was not asking me to judge all the nations of the world, or to elucidate all the moral and political motives behind their actions. He was not demanding that I pass some critical decision defining the innocence and guilt of all those concerned in the war. He was asking me to make a choice that amounted to an act of love for His truth, His goodness, His charity, His Gospel. ... He was asking me to do, to the best of my knowledge, what I thought Christ would do. ... After all, Christ did say, "Whatsoever you have done to the least of these my brethren, you did it to me."[137]

When he took his army physical, it turned out he was unsuitable for military service of any kind, with or without a gun. Soldiers had to have a certain number of teeth. Merton's encounters with dentists had left him short. He was classified 1-B. Only 1-As were being drafted.

No room in the seminary: his student sins and their consequences too enduring. No room on the battlefield: too many morals, too few teeth.

With his images of the future abruptly altered, Merton found himself thinking about a battlefield of a different sort, the Trappist monastery in Kentucky. This would be a good place, he decided, to spend the Easter recess. He reached the abbey on the eve of Palm Sunday, April 5.

# Gethsemani and Harlem

*This is the center of America.*

It was Holy Week, 1941. Huge areas of London were devastated. Coventry had been razed. The country where Merton had lived so much of his life had become a land of blood and smoke.

Events that convinced others to go to war pushed Merton in the opposite direction. He believed that what Hitler represented could not be defeated by the methods the Nazis relied on: intimidation, violence, and murder. The only adequate response to evil, Merton was certain, was sanctity. "There is only one defense: to take the Gospel literally, and to be *saints*."[138]

Fresh from his decision not to take part in bloodshed, Merton arrived at the Abbey of Gethsemani to share in monastic recollection of the crucifixion of Christ and to participate in his resurrection.

Unpacking his suitcase in the monastery guest house, Merton was overwhelmed with the sense that he had finally found the center he was looking for. "I should tear out all the pages of this book," he wrote in his journal, "and all the other pages of anything else I have ever written, and begin here. This is the center of America. I had wondered what was holding the country together, what has been keeping the universe from cracking in pieces and falling apart. It is places like this monastery—not only this one: there must be others."[139]

On Holy Saturday, five days later, he confided: "I desire only one thing: to love God. Those who love

Below:
The center of Harlem, 125th St., in the 1940's. (Photograph courtesy of the Schomburg Center, New York City Public Library)

[73]

him keep his commandments. I only desire to do one thing: to follow his will. I pray that I am at least beginning to know what that may mean. Could it possibly mean that I might someday become a monk in this monastery? My Lord, and my King, and my God!"[140]

Yet there was the obvious counter-question: If his past was such that he was unacceptable to the Franciscans, would not the Trappists have similar objections?

Easter Monday, returning to the non-monastic world, he felt more than ever like an outsider. He noticed that even women's clothing was being drawn into the war, military insignia being added for decorative touches. The big news was the German army landing in Egypt.

Back at St. Bonaventure's to teach Dante at summer school, another vocational possibility was opened to Merton by a visiting speaker: Catherine de Hueck Doherty, nicknamed the Baroness because she had been born into an aristocratic Russian family. She described a project she had founded, Friendship House, a lay Catholic community in Harlem—black territory where few whites dared to be seen—that was trying to put into practice the church's teaching about social justice. A plain-speaking woman, the Baroness responded to a priest's objections with the word, "Baloney!" Merton was impressed with the way she spoke of martyrdom without embarrassment. "The way she said some things . . . left you ready to do some kind of action . . . renounce the world, live in total poverty, but also doing very definite things: ministering to the poor in a certain definite way."[141]

When she mentioned that she was looking for someone to help with clothing distribution, Merton volunteered.

As a student at Columbia, Merton had lived for years just across the border from Harlem without fully seeing what was there or understanding what a

Above:
Catherine de Hueck (center), founder of Friendship House in Harlem. (Photograph courtesy of Boston College, Burns Library)

*"She and those who joined her . . . would live and work in the slums, lose themselves, in the huge anonymous mass of the forgotten and the derelict, for the only purpose of living the complete, integral Christian life in that environment—loving those around them, sacrificing themselves for those around them, spreading the Gospel and the truth of Christ most of all by being saints, by living in union with Him, by being full of His Holy Ghost, His Charity."*
(The Seven Storey Mountain)

ghetto meant. Now that he was spending time every week at Friendship House on 135th Street at Lenox Avenue, he was aware of the mortal sin of racism. Because of skin color, millions of people were regarded as less than human and were even driven to regard themselves that way. He saw Harlem as a "divine indictment against New York City and the people who live downtown and make their money downtown."[142]

Merton's sense of outrage at what ghettoes represented never cooled:

Here in this huge, dark, steaming slum, hundreds of thousands of Negroes are herded together like cattle, most of them with little to eat and nothing to do. All the senses and imagination and sensibilities and emotions and sorrows and desires and hopes and ideas of a race with vivid feelings and deep emotional

Below:
Friendship House, an urban center run by a lay Catholic community on 135th St. in Harlem, where Merton worked for a short time in 1941.

reactions are forced in upon themselves, bound inward by an iron ring of frustration: the prejudice that hems them in with its four insurmountable walls. In this huge cauldron inestimable natural gifts, wisdom, love, music, science, poetry, are stamped down and left to boil . . . and thousands upon thousands of souls are destroyed.[143]

Yet, despite all the evidence of social destruction and ruined lives, Merton was dazzled by Harlem's beauty, in the children most of all, but also in the old. He remembered one aged woman sitting on the steps of Friendship House on a hot summer evening. "I saw in this tired, serene and holy face the patience and joy of the martyrs and the clear, unquenchable light of sanctity . . . a deep, unfathomable, shining peace."[144]

The faith of Friendship House's small volunteer community and the welcome he found in Harlem made Merton reconsider his vocation. Sipping black Russian tea with the Baroness, he talked about making Harlem his home and this work his life. Such a choice had the additional advantage that he would remain free to write, which he expected would be forbidden by the Trappists. On the other hand, the attraction to Gethsemani continued with growing intensity.

On retreat for five days in early September at the Trappist Monastery of Our Lady of the Valley near Providence, Rhode Island, he wrestled with the choices, struggling to understand his own motives. Writing about his quandary to the Baroness, he described himself as being tied up like a pretzel. Reading the story of the rich young man whom Jesus had called to give up everything "half kills me," he told Mark Van Doren.[145]

In his room at St. Bonaventure's on the night of November 27, Merton wrote in his journal, "Should I be going to Harlem, or to the Trappists? Why

"I don't know if you are concerned about the past of people who come to work for you. I am bringing this up because it might possibly be important. I got in some trouble once, which I don't particularly want to tell anybody about. If you absolutely want to know, I will tell you, but otherwise I can say in good conscience that I don't believe, myself, that it would disqualify me from working in Friendship House . . . [though it was] enough for it to be an impediment to my becoming a priest . . . It is something that definitely demands a whole life of penance and absolute self-sacrifice: so that if I thought the Trappists would take me, I think I would want to go to them. But I have to do penance, and if Harlem won't have me, then where may I turn?"
(Letter to Catherine de Hueck, November 10, 1941)

doesn't this idea of the Trappists leave me? Perhaps what I am afraid of is to write and be rejected. . . . Perhaps I cling to my independence, to the chance to write, to go where I like in the world. . . . Going to live in Harlem . . . is a good and reasonable way to follow Christ. But going to the Trappists is exciting, it fills me with awe and desire. I return to the idea again and again: 'Give up *everything*, give up *everything*!' "146

He talked with Father Philotheus, one of the friars, about his attraction to the Trappists and asked the burning question: whether having fathered a child was an absolute impediment to the priesthood. Father Philotheus said that, in his opinion, there was no insurmountable obstacle and suggested

Below:
Harlem in the 1940s. (Photograph courtesy of the Schomburg Center, New York City Public Library)

that Merton's next step would be to go to Gethsemani during Christmas vacation to talk about the problem with the Abbot.

"I rushed out of [Father Philotheus's] room," Merton wrote to the Baroness on December 6, "saying all I could remember of the *Te Deum* and went and fell on my face in the chapel and began to pray and beg and implore Almighty God to let me be admitted to the Trappists."[147]

Leaving the chapel, he was at last ready to risk another rejection. That night he wrote to the Abbot of Gethsemani. A few days later the Abbot responded with permission to come.

Along with the Abbot's note came a letter from the draft board summoning Merton to appear for a second physical examination; the rule about teeth had changed and he was probably 1-A, suitable for immediate drafting. Merton convinced the draft board to delay the physical while he was at the monastery, wrote to the Abbot to ask if he could come sooner than planned, and started giving away his possessions: his manuscripts to Mark Van Doren, his journal to Catherine de Hueck Doherty, his clothes to Friendship House, his books to the university library. All he retained was a Bible, breviary, a copy of *The Imitation of Christ*, a volume of Saint John of the Cross, a collection of Gerard Manley Hopkins's poems, an anthology of William Blake, the minimum clothing needed for a one-day trip, and a rosary.

It was time, he told Bob Lax, "to get out of the subway and go into the clean woods."[148]

On December 9, the day after Congress declared war on Japan, Merton closed his bank account. On December 10 he travelled by train to the Court of the Queen of Heaven in Kentucky.

Above:
The shrine of St. Therese of Lisieux, the "Little Flower," at the St. Bonaventure campus. Merton was praying before this shrine when he decided to apply for admission to the Abbey of Gethsemani. (Photograph by F. Donald Kenney, courtesy of St. Bonaventure University)

*"I don't think there was ever a moment in my life when my soul felt so urgent and special an anguish ... 'Please help me. What am I going to do? I can't go on like this.' Suddenly, as soon as I had made the prayer, I became aware of the wood, the trees, the dark hills, the wet night wind, and then, clearer than any of these obvious realities, in my imagination, I began to hear the great bell of Gethsemani ringing in the night ... The bell seemed to be telling me where I belonged — as if it were calling me home ..."*
(The Seven Storey Mountain)

# Brother Louis

*Everything I wanted to do the most, I can now try to do all the time without any interference. . . . As soon as I got inside, I knew I was home, where I never had been or would be a stranger.*

O̲n December 13 Merton was interviewed by the Abbot, Dom Frederic Dunne, and was accepted as a postulant choir monk: a member of the community who participates in singing the daily "offices" of prayer and is being prepared for ordination as a priest. On February 21, 1942, his head shaved, he put on the white robes of a novice. Signifying the transition, he was given a new name: Frater Maria Ludovicus—Brother Mary Louis. All Trappists took Mary as a first name; she was the order's patroness. Merton's particular namesake, Louis, was the crusader king of France who had ruled in the thirteenth century. The name seemed apt for a French-born novice. The Abbot, suffering pneumonia at the time, gave the newly vested novices an impassioned warning that they had nothing to look forward to but sickness, sorrows, humiliations, fasts, and everything human nature hates: the cross.

Changes in recent years have softened many of the sharp edges in Trappist life as Merton found it. A monk of Gethsemani today has his own small room, freedom to correspond and to follow world news, and warmth in the winter. The life Merton embraced in 1941 was more austere. The monks slept in their robes on straw-covered boards in dormitories that were frigid in winter and sweltering in

Below:
Spire of the Abbey of Gethsemani in winter. (Photograph courtesy of Boston College, Burns Library)

*"Suddenly I saw a steeple that shone like silver in the moonlight, growing into sight from behind a rounded knoll . . . Breathless, I looked at the monastery that was revealed before me as we came over the rise."*
(The Seven Storey Mountain)

summer. Beds were separated by shoulder-high partitions. Half the year was fasting time. A typical meal featured bread, potatoes, an apple, and barley coffee. Even on such "feast days" as Easter and Christmas, meat, fish, and eggs were never served. There were, and still are, long hours of communal prayer in the church: about eight hours a day. In those days the fire wasn't lit until frost had iced the church windows. Trappist underwear was still of fifteenth-century design. Hot water was on tap two days a week. To chastise their flesh still further, there was the "discipline"—a small whip with which each monk lashed his bare back on Fridays while sitting on his bed and reciting the Our Father. Infractions of the rule were denounced in public, at the Chapter of Faults. A novice's few personal possessions were kept in a small box in the scriptorium. Hard manual labor was done with tools that had changed little since medieval times. News from the outside world rarely reached the monks. Communication was mainly by sign language using four hundred hand gestures that mainly had to do with prayer, labor, and food. Barring special permission, mail to the outside world could be sent only four times a year: Easter, Assumption, All Saints, and Christmas, and then only four half-page letters, all of which were read by a superior before being posted. Delivery of mail was normally restricted to the same four feasts.

The choir novices attended four or five classes a week: study of the Benedictine Rule, spiritual life, liturgy, and singing were the primary subjects. The novice had occasional private conferences with the Novice Master plus infrequent meetings with the Abbot. There were a few hours of labor each day, farm work, cleaning, or cutting lumber. While the word solitude was often used to describe Trappist life, privacy was practically nonexistent.

It wasn't easy for Merton. He wasn't robust, treasured privacy, and he didn't like the smell of straw. But he took to Trappist life and tradition with joy. Far from feeling imprisoned, he felt free. The monastery was the one place in the world, he wrote on the anniversary of his first visit, "where everything makes sense. . . . Everything I wanted to do the most, I can now try to do all the time without any interference. . . . As soon as I got inside, I knew I was home, where I never had been or would be a stranger."

Though there were periods of difficulty and uncertainty, times of frustration with the demands and intrusions of community life, his writings in the first few years mainly record a life of confidence, growth, and a sense of God's presence. "What a life," he wrote Mark Van Doren in April 1942. "It is tremendous. Not because of any acts we perform, any penance, any single feature of the liturgy or the chant, not because we sleep on boards & straw mattresses & fast & work & sweat & sing & keep silence. These things are all utterly simple acts that have no importance whatever in themselves. But the whole unity of the life *is* tremendous. . . . The life is a real unity. . . . The foundation of its unity is God's unity. . . . His *simplicity is* our life. We *live* His oneness: we *live* his singleness of concentration. . . . No wonder it is wonderful. The life is God . . . Christ is the principle & end of absolutely everything that a Trappist does, right down to breathing."[149]

"What surprises me," he wrote Lax in November, "is not that I am happy here but that I ever tried to fool myself I was happy anywhere else." He described Mass as a "solemn & complicated drama of angels" with the words of Mass proclaiming "the infinite kindness of God." He told Lax about his fellow monks, in whom he found the "same proportion of people with faces that frighten you as everywhere else. The men who come here are the same, originally, as the men in the subway. . . . But the difference is, here they have forgotten about being wise guys. . . . A lot of my brothers are really saints. . . . The thing that makes the most sense," he concluded, "is to be in the presence of God & live by His will as we live on air & bread."[150]

In his poems and journal writings from his first years in the monastery one often finds a wild joy that he is among exiles: monks who had escaped the world of war and oppression, ambition and competition. The monastery remains a kind of rough paradise. Yet a sense of connection with those who haven't escaped the subway world remains. In a letter that first year he told his friends, "We pray all night in tears for people who are being hit and kicked and killed, and who cannot help it."

One of those killed was Merton's brother, John Paul, who had joined the Royal Canadian Air Force. The two brothers, whose lives had so often taken

Above:
Thomas Merton in his early years as a monk. (Photograph courtesy of Boston College, Burns Library)

them in opposite directions, had grown closer when Tom returned from England and entered Columbia, though the closeness had more to do with going to the movies than sharing a religious transformation. It wasn't until John Paul was in uniform that he followed his brother into the church. By then he was a Sergeant Observer, trained to be part of a bomber crew, thus to participate in the kind of military activity, aerial warfare, that most troubled his older brother. Yet the bond between them was becoming deeper. Finishing his initial military training and before going to England to join a bombing squadron, in July 1942 John Paul came to Gethsemani to visit Tom and ended up being baptized. For four days leading up to the event, Tom instructed John Paul in the basics of Catholic Christianity.

Yet even with this new line of connection, there remained separation. In one of the more poignant scenes in *The Seven Storey Mountain*, we witness

Below:
Monks in choir. (Photograph courtesy of the Abbey of Gethsemani)

*"Practically the first thing you noticed, when you looked at the choir, was this young man in secular clothes, among all the monks. Then suddenly we saw him no more. He was in white. They had given him an oblate's habit, and you could not pick him out from the rest. The waters had closed over his head, and he was submerged in the community. He was lost. The world would hear of him no more. He had drowned to our society and become a Cistercian."*
(The Seven Storey Mountain)

Merton trying, by sign language, to invite his brother down from the church loft to be with him: "John Paul was kneeling all alone, in uniform. He seemed to be an immense distance away." Between them was a locked door. Merton couldn't call up to tell him the way around it through the guest house. He resorted to sign language, but John Paul didn't understand the signs. "At that moment there flashed into my mind all the scores of times in our ... childhood when I had chased John Paul away with stones. ... And now, all of a sudden, here it was all over again ... John Paul, standing, confused and unhappy, at a distance which he was not able to bridge."[151]

Nine months later, during Lent 1943, a telegram arrived at Gethsemani reporting that Sergeant J. P. Merton was missing in action. A death notice followed. Later came details of John Paul's last days.

His bomber had been shot down over the North
Sea. Though badly wounded, John Paul survived
with other crew members, floating in a rubber raft.
He died on the fourth day and was buried at sea.

The pacifist monk wrote a poem to his soldier
brother offering him his monastic life:

Sweet brother, if I do not sleep
My eyes are flowers for your tomb;
And if I cannot eat my bread,
My fasts shall live like willows where you died.
If in the heat I find no water for my thirst,
My thirst shall turn to springs for you, poor
    traveller. . . .

Come, in my labor find a resting place
And in my sorrows lay your head,
Or rather take my life and blood
And buy yourself a better bed —
Or take my breath and take my death
And buy yourself a better rest.

When all the men of war are shot
And flags have fallen into dust,
Your cross and mine shall tell men still
Christ died on each, for both of us.

For in the wreckage of your April Christ lies
    slain,
And Christ weeps in the ruins of my spring:
The money of Whose tears shall fall
Into your weak and friendless hand,
And buy you back to your own land:
The silence of Whose tears shall fall
Like bells upon your alien tomb.
Hear them and come: they call you home.[152]

Parents, grandparents, and brother dead, a sole
survivor, Merton went deeper into monastic life.
March 19, 1944, he took simple vows committing
himself to three more years of testing before final
vows.

# Thomas Merton
# vs. Brother Louis

*Nobody seems to understand that one of us has got to die.*

Entering Gethsemani, Merton had intended to sacrifice his aspirations as a writer and "to disappear into God."[153] He was terrified of his ambition to be noticed, to be influential, to have a name, to become famous. Yet his compulsion to write wouldn't go away. He kept a journal from his first day at Gethsemani, and soon there were poems.

In the final pages of *The Seven Storey Mountain* Merton refers to his writer-self as a shadow who had followed him into the cloister, an enemy named Thomas Merton. "Nobody seems to understand that one of us has got to die."[154] One of the hardest tests of his vow of obedience was to lay aside his own will on the matter. The test of not writing may have been even harder. In the complex contest with himself, the writer side won steadily. But God must have had a writer in mind from the beginning.

Merton knew that Trappists were suspicious of intellectual work, but Dom Frederic, the son of a bookbinder and publisher, loved books and had already arranged publication by an older monk, Father Raymond. While aware of the novice's mixed feelings about writing, Dom Frederic encouraged Merton to continue with his poetry and began assigning him to various writing projects. Merton

Opposite:
Thomas Merton in 1949, around the time that *The Seven Storey Mountain* was first published. (Photograph courtesy of the Abbey of Gethsemani)

*"In one sense we are always travelling, and travelling as if we did not know where we were going. In another sense we have already arrived."*

(The Seven Storey Mountain)

[87]

resisted periodically, on one occasion appealing to the Order's Abbot General. It was in vain. While there was a brief period when his confessor ordered him to stop writing poems, the Abbot decided otherwise. His superiors believed that Merton had a gift from God that was useful to the community and recognized an obligation to help in its nurturing.

In 1942 one of his poems appeared in *The New Yorker* and four in *Poetry*. His first book, *Thirty Poems*, was published by James Laughlin of New Directions in 1944, and a second, *A Man in the Divided Sea*, appeared two years later. Seven more collections followed, ending posthumously with the Bible-sized *Collected Poems*. (While preparing *A Man in the Divided Sea*, Merton received orders that only his secular name was to appear with his book and that no author photo was permitted. The ruling stood for the rest of his life. For many years few readers had any idea what Merton looked like.)

While a novice, Merton had disclosed the temptation to write his life story; his confessor laughed. In March 1946 Dom Frederic encouraged Merton to write an autobiography. In a letter to James Laughlin, Merton described the book-to-be as "a cross between Dante's Purgatory, and Kafka, and a medieval miracle play."[155] The title, already in his mind, was taken from Dante's image of purgatory: *The Seven Storey Mountain*. In May 1946 Merton gave Dom Frederic a memorandum (intended for the order's General Chapter, it was written in the third person) in which Merton listed various books he was prepared to write in the coming years and for which he sought the order's blessing: works on Trappist history, biographies of Cistercian saints, a book on contemplation, another on monastic community life, and a study of ancient Cistercian liturgy. The final item on the three-page list was "a biography . . . of a Gethsemani monk" who was the "son of artists, was born in Europe, and passed through the abyss of communism and modern-day university life before being led to the cloister by the merciful love of Jesus."[156]

Above:
Cover of *A Man in the Divided Sea*, published in 1946 by New Directions.

*If on Your Cross Your life and death and mine*
*   are one,*
*Loves teaches me to read, in You, the rest of a*
*   new history.*
*I trace my days back to another childhood . . .*
*Until I find a manger, star and straw,*
*A pair of animals, some simple men,*
*And thus I learn that I was born,*
*Now not in France, but Bethlehem."*
                                    *("The Biography")*

With Dom Frederic's backing and his own reservations about being a writer temporarily dismissed, Merton threw his considerable energies into the autobiography. Kafka, miracle plays, even Dante all fell to the side in favor of straight-forward narrative. True to its title, however, the manuscript was becoming mountain-sized: "I cannot make it less than 650 typewritten pages," Merton wrote Laughlin in August.[157]

In late October 1946, Merton sent the manuscript to his agent, Naomi Burton. Weeks passed before she had time to read it. In December she gave it to Robert Giroux. Having gone from Columbia into the Navy, Giroux was now an editor at Harcourt, Brace in New York. Assured by Giroux that the book was not likely to lose money, the company agreed to sign a contract with Merton. "MANUSCRIPT ACCEPTED," Giroux telegraphed Merton. "HAPPY NEW YEAR."

The good news was followed by bad. In the spring of 1947 one of the order's censors nearly blocked publication. On top of objections to the sex and drinking in the original text, he was irritated by the prose style; he suggested Merton take a correspondence course in English grammar before attempting any more books. Rounds of editing and rewriting were required that veiled the more controversial events in Merton's earlier life and delayed the book's publication until 1948 — October 4, as it happened, the feast of Saint Francis of Assisi.

"It did not seem to me, nor to anyone in the firm," Giroux recalled, "that it would become a national phenomenon. It merely looked as if the book would 'do all right.' "[158] The first printing was 7,500 copies. The book's prepublication sale — 20,847 copies — already suggested that the book was going to sell. A second printing of 20,000 copies was needed prior to the official publication day. In October, orders for 5,900 more copies were received, in November 13,000, in December 31,000. On one record day, 10,000 copies were ordered. In May 1949 Giroux

*"At work — writing — I am doing a little better. I mean, I am less tied up in it, more peaceful and more detached . . . Meanwhile, for myself, I have only one desire and that is the desire for solitude — to disappear into God, to be submerged in His peace, to be lost in the secret of His face."*

(The Sign of Jonas)

[89]

hand-delivered copy number 100,000, specially bound in leather, as a gift for the author. The original cloth edition of *The Seven Storey Mountain* sold more than 600,000 copies, while in paperback sales the figure went into the millions. The book has been continually in print since 1948. A British edition followed: *Elected Silence*, edited and with a foreword by Evelyn Waugh. Translations eventually appeared in sixteen languages. Merton wondered if Gary Cooper would play the leading role if the book ended up in Hollywood.[159] (In fact film offers eventually were made for the book, but the Abbot and Merton were of one mind about turning them down.)

What was behind the book's remarkable popularity? Partly it was the merits of an extraordinary story told by a writer who played words as freely as Charlie Parker played the saxophone. Partly it was timing. Readers were ready to listen to Merton's radical criticism of a social order which a few years before had seemed worth killing and dying for. Obliteration bombing of cities by the allies had produced millions of civilian casualties; the Germans and Japanese were not alone in their guilt. "Everything should have been changed by the awful war," said Giroux, "but it became pretty clear by 1947 that nothing at all was changing, in fact it was going to start all over again."[160]

Still more important was Merton's contagious enthusiasm for the life of faith, voluntary poverty, penance, and prayer, and his passionate confession of the mercy of God. *The Seven Storey Mountain* was an electrifying challenge to the idea that human happiness consists mainly of a proper diet, a good job, a comfortable address, and an active sex life.

The book had its shortcomings: sarcastic stabs at non-Catholic Christianity, condescension in describing Catholic religious communities less rigorous than the Trappists, and the suggestion that those who really wanted to reach the high wire of holiness would end up monks. Later in life Merton was dismayed at how narrow and judgmental he had been. Yet the strengths of

Below:
Cover of the mass-market paperback edition of *The Seven Storey Mountain*.

"*The Seven Storey Mountain* is the work of a man I never even heard of."
(The Sign of Jonas)

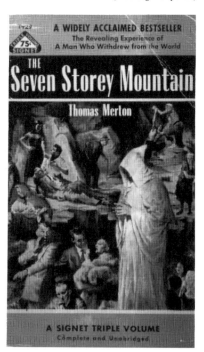

[90]

the book easily outweigh its weaknesses. *The Seven Storey Mountain* remains one of the most compelling conversion stories ever written.

The significance of the book for its readers was registered not only in sales. Stacks of letters were sent to Merton, far too many to answer. He was forced to respond with printed messages produced on the monastery press. His fame worried him and deepened his doubts about the advisability of writing.

Yet the writing continued. A new book of poems, *Figures for an Apocalypse*, came out in 1947 and was well received, but *Exile Ends in Glory*, a biography of Mother Berchmans, OCSO, was quickly and mercifully forgotten. *The Waters of Siloe*, a history of the Trappists published in 1949, remains good reading. The same year produced another book of poetry, *Tears of the Blind Lions*, and *Seeds of Contemplation*, a collection of brief meditations that went through many printings and translations. *What Are These Wounds?*, a biography of Saint Lutagarde, was issued in 1950; written while Merton was in the novitiate, it is an example of sugar-coated Catholic piety at its most cloying.

His books were selling well and some have stood the test of years, but Merton found each of them troubling. "Where did I get all that pious rhetoric?" Merton wondered when he had to suffer through the public reading of *Exile Ends in Glory* during meals. "[The book] is one of the worst pieces of cheese that has ever been served in our rectory."[161] Even *Seeds of Contemplation*, a much better book, distressed him. "It lacks warmth and human affection," he noted in his journal.[162] Parts of *The Waters of Siloe* struck him as "impertinent."[163] Correcting page proofs for *Figures for an Apocalypse*, Merton found himself disgusted.[164]

"A bad book about the love of God," he scolded himself, "remains a bad book."[165]

Above:
Cover of *Figures for an Apocalypse*, published in 1948 by New Directions.

*Go, stubborn talker,*
*Find you a station on the loud world's corners,*
*And try there (if your hands be clean) your*
*    length of patience;*
*Use there the rhythms that upset my sickness,*
*And spend your pennyworth of prayer*
*There in the clamor of the Christless avenues.*

*And try to ransom some one prisoner.*
*Out of those walls, of traffic, out of the wheels*
*    of that unhappiness.*
*                ("The Poet, To His Book")*

# Vows

*God has leavened the whole world with apostles that He scraped off pots in the kitchens of the Greeks.*

Having written an autobiography that presented monastic life in general and Trappist life in particular in the best possible light, once the book was finished Merton found he was overwhelmed by distractions when singing in choir and was losing all sense of the presence of God. He was troubled by the heavy work load, one day listing in his journal twelve books and booklets that he was supposed to be writing. He suffered from insomnia and experienced growing doubts about whether he really belonged with the Trappists.

The Carthusians were often in his thoughts: a way of monastic life that provided a high degree of individual privacy; Carthusian monks were hermits within community. The Trappists, it seemed to Merton, had practically abolished privacy and with it much of the climate of contemplative life. In a moment of exasperation following difficulties with the order's censors, he opened fire on the Trappist sweat ethic: "Trappists believe that everything that costs them is God's will. Anything that makes you suffer is God's will. If it makes you sweat, it is God's will. But we have serious doubts about the things which demand no expense of physical energy. . . . We think we have done great things because we are worn out."[166] In his darker moments Merton wished he had been aware of the Carthusians when he was

Opposite:
Merton is ordained as Father M. Louis, O.C.S.O., May 26, 1949, the Feast of the Ascension. (Photograph courtesy of the Thomas Merton Studies Center)

[93]

choosing between Friendship House and Gethsemani.

Part of the problem he was struggling to resolve within himself was a recurrent vagrant itch: "There is something in my nature," he wrote early in 1949, "that makes me dream of being a tramp." He thought longingly of flea-inhabited holy wanderers like Saint Benedict Joseph Labré. He found himself "woefully respectable."[167] He was feeling like "a duck in a chicken coop."[168]

His Abbot and his confessor both argued that God had brought him to Gethsemani and intended for him to remain, and most of the time Merton agreed. In January 1947, shortly before taking final vows, Merton wrote:

> It is really illogical that I should get temptations to run off to [the Carthusian] Order. . . . God has put me in a place where I can spend hour after hour, each day, in occupations that are always on the borderline of prayer. There is always a chance to step over the line and enter into simple and contemplative union with God. . . . I am such a fool that I consent to imagine that in some other situation I would quickly advance to a high degree of prayer. . . . [God] has put me in this place . . . and if He ever wants to put me anywhere else, He will do so in a way that will leave no doubt as to who is doing it.[169]

"The important thing is not to live for contemplation but to live for God," he reminded himself. "As soon as you stop travelling, you have arrived."[170]

On the feast of Saint Joseph, March 19, 1947, Merton made a lifetime commitment to poverty, chastity, obedience, continuing conversion, and stability, all in the context of the Abbey of Gethsemani. The vows were heartfelt and considered, but they didn't dismiss the doubts. Months after final

*Where, on what cross my agony will come*
*I do not ask You:*
*For it is written and accomplished here,*
*On every Crucifix, on every altar.*
*It is my narrative that drowns and is forgotten*

*In Your five open Jordans,*
*Your voice that cries my: "Consummatum est."*
　　　　　　　　　　　　　　　　　*("The Biography")*

vows, he was embarrassed to be found in the library by a brother monk "*in flagrante delicto*, ravished by the pictures of all the [Carthusian] Charterhouses that existed at the end of the last century."[171] News that a noted Benedictine monk had become a Carthusian filled Merton with envy, but he sensed that his infatuation with Charterhouses didn't spring from his conscience.

Aware that Merton was finding it nearly impossible to sleep in the dormitory, Dom Frederic had let him use a small room over the stairs, thus giving Merton a small degree of the solitude he sought more and more urgently. Merton's health bothered him, yet he found there was a blessing in sickness: the contemplative leisure that came with being a patient in the infirmary. "As soon as I get into a cell by myself I am a different person," he wrote in his journal during an infirmary stay. "Prayer becomes what it ought to be. . . . To have nothing to do but abandon yourself to God. . . . Plenty of time. No manuscripts, no typewriter, no rushing back and forth to church, no scriptorium, no breaking your neck to get things done before the next thing happens."[172]

Death had robbed Merton of his parents; during his seventh year at Gethsemani, death withdrew a spiritual father. Dom Frederic died on August 4, 1948, though having lived long enough to hand Merton the first copy of *The Seven Storey Mountain*. His final advice to Merton had been to go on writing in order "to make people love the spiritual life."[173] Merton couldn't recall anyone who had ever been kinder to him, and marveled at the Abbot's patience.

Below:
Several Trappist novices gather wood near the Abbey. (Photograph courtesy of Boston College, Burns Library)

*"In January the novices were working in the woods near the lake . . . The woods were quiet and the axes echoed . . . You are not supposed to pause and pray when you are at work. American Trappist notions of contemplation do not extend to that . . . But that January, I was still so new that I had not yet flung myself into that complex and absurd system of meditation . . . And occasionally I looked up through the trees to where the spire of the abbey church rose up in the distance, and I thought of a line from one of the gradual psalms: 'The Lord is round about His people from henceforth, now and forever.' It was true."*

(The Seven Storey Mountain)

Problems Merton had been complaining to Dom Frederic about while he was still alive went into recess after the abbot's death, as if the old monk had carried them with him to heaven. In September 1948 Merton described a deep sense of joy and at-homeness in the monastery: "Love sails me around the house. I walk two steps in the ground and four steps in the air. It is love. It is consolation. . . . Love is pushing me around the monastery, love is kicking me all around like a gong I tell you, love is the only thing that makes it possible for me to continue to tick."[174]

The elation didn't last long. By the following February Merton found that something within him seemed to have dried up and that he was hardly able to write. He felt tied up in knots.[175] "I would laboriously cover fifty pages with typescript and then tear them all up and start over again."[176] The book he was struggling with, finally published in 1951 as *The Ascent to Truth*, was a presentation of the spirituality of Saint John of the Cross, Merton's favorite mystic, whose dark path was Merton's as well. "We must always walk in darkness," Merton wrote in one of the book's most glowing passages. "We must travel in silence. We must fly by night." But the book as a whole showed the signs of the author's condition during much of the time he was writing it; it was labored, academic, and dry.

Preoccupation with impending ordination was contributing to his immobility. There were the occasional flare-ups of his Carthusian enchantment, often in tandem with irritation with life at Gethsemani. He felt wrung out by the books already written and was embarrassed, at times revolted, by his fame. He was also trying to cope with the letters addressed to him, many of which required personal replies rather than printed cards. There were demands on his time and energy from important visitors, among them Evelyn Waugh, who told Merton that he should improve his punctuation and edit his work far more

*"The world is terrible, people are starving to death and freezing and going to hell with despair and here I sit with a silver spoon in my mouth and write books and everybody sends me fan mail telling me how wonderful I am for giving up so much. I'd like to ask them, what have I given up, anyway, except headaches and responsibilities?"*

(The Sign of Jonas)

severely. On top of everything else, Merton felt so discouraged by his work as a poet that for a time he gave up writing poems. Only his journal-writing seemed to go easily, perhaps because it wasn't intended for publication. At the end of January 1949 he wondered if he were finished as a writer. "Far from disturbing me, the thought made me glad."[177]

Another factor contributing to the uncertainty in Merton's life at the time was Dom James Fox, the new Abbot. With his election, Dom James became responsible for the care and feeding of two hundred monks, the enlargement of space to better accommodate so large a community, and the repair of buildings that were nearly derelict. The abbey's income, mainly from Mass stipends and contributions, wasn't nearly enough. Dom James was determined to make the farming profitable and to find other ways to make the abbey solvent. A graduate of the Harvard Business School and subscriber to *The Wall Street Journal*, he was well prepared for the task, but was not the kind of person Merton easily warmed to. The Abbot's businesslike new regime irritated Merton while the increasing reliance on noisy farm machinery afflicted his ears. Merton had thought he was leaving factory clamor behind when he fled to Gethsemani.

Merton's ordination to the priesthood had been twice delayed, first at the suggestion of his confessor, then because of Dom Frederic's death. Dom James was ready to proceed, but first demanded a formal declaration that he didn't intend to become a Carthusian, a promise Merton provided. To reassure Merton of his respect for Merton's needs, Dom James designated the monastery's rare book vault — one of the few places in the abbey that was both silent and solitary — as Merton's new place to work.

On March 19, 1949, the feast of Saint Joseph once again, Merton was ordained a deacon. Serving at Benediction the next day, he felt all in a fog but very happy. "All I could think about was picking up

*"The truest solitude is not something outside you, not an absence of men or of sound around you; it is an abyss opening up in the center of your own soul. And this abyss of interior solitude is created by a hunger that will never be satisfied with any created things."*
(Seeds of Contemplation)

the Host [bread that had become the Body of Christ]. I was afraid the whole Church would come down on my head, because of what I used to be."[178] His sense of awe that he would soon preside at the liturgy deepened each day. "It seems to me impossible that I should live the next two and a half weeks without keeling over," he noted on May 8.[179]

The transition from Brother Louis to Father Louis took place on the feast of the Ascension, May 26. As Merton lay on the stone floor of the abbey church, he was overcome not with tears but laughter, as if to say: *How funny God is choosing someone like me for something like this!*

"Even my past sins fit into the picture," he reflected in a letter to Sister Therese Lentfoehr, "throwing into high relief the tremendous mercy of God."[180] The priesthood, Merton told Mark Van Doren, would give him a completely social function that he had always been trying to escape. "Actually,

Below:
Merton's ordination in the Abbey Chapel at Gethsemani. (Photograph courtesy of the Abbey of Gethsemani)

*"My priestly ordination was, I felt, the one great secret for which I had been born. Ten years before I was ordained, and seemed to be one of the men in the world most unlikely to become a priest, I had suddenly realized that for me ordination to the priesthood was, in fact, a matter of life or death . . . "*

(The Sign of Jonas)

having run into it at this end of the circle, it is making me what I was always meant to be."[181]

Asked afterward if he had been nervous during the ordination, Merton replied in Trappist sign language, making a circle with thumb and forefinger, then using the forefinger of his left hand to make a center point, a silent declaration that he was finally at the place of convergence he had long been seeking.

Merton's ordination turned into a three-day homecoming festival. Friends he hadn't seen in years gathered at the monastery to share in the event and participate in his first Masses: Bob Lax, Ed Rice, Dan Walsh, Bob Giroux, Jay Laughlin, and Sy Freedgood. "In the end I had the impression that all who came to see me were dispersing to the four corners of the universe with hymns and messages and prophecies, speaking with tongues and ready to raise the dead."[182]

Among those raised from the dead was the man himself. Ordained at last, he was able to reconcile Father Louis, monk, and Thomas Merton, writer.

"My lamentations about my writing job have been foolish," he noted in his journal in July. "Writing is the one thing that gives me access to some real silence and solitude. Also I find that it helps me to pray because when I pause at my work I find that the mirror inside me is surprisingly clean and deep and serene and God shines there and is immediately found, without hunting, as if He had come close to me while I was writing and I had not observed His coming."[183] "My [writing] work is my hermitage," he noted six months later, "because it is *writing* that helps me most of all to be a solitary and a contemplative here at Gethsemani."[184]

Below:
Merton as a young monk. (Photograph courtesy of the Abbey of Gethsemani)

*"The Christian life — and especially the contemplative life — is a continual discovery of Christ in new and unexpected places."*
(The Sign of Jonas)

# In the Belly of a Whale

*God is in His transparent world, but He is too sacred to be mentioned, too holy to be observed. The big deep fish are purple in my sea.*

"All for Jesus, through Mary, with a smile." This was Dom James's motto, not Merton's. Merton was forever fleeing from slogans, religious ones most of all. He found Dom James's smiles galling and was often irritated with the Abbot's sermons. "Jesus must be our real pal," Dom James told the monks, "our most intimate buddy."[185] The Christ to whom Merton was drawn, far from being a potential pal, was the Christ of the Icons: the Christ of the Transfiguration.

Yet Merton repeatedly admitted that he needed Dom James. For all the differences in theology and personality between superior and subordinate, and all the familial combat between them, there was profound mutual respect. While expressing themselves in dissimilar voices, both were profoundly committed to the church and the monastic life, and neither viewed these in static terms. Merton recognized Dom James as an authentic pastor, not seeing monks as interchangeable parts but aware of each person as original and thus requiring unique responses and attention. (For a member of the community who was obsessed with flowers, Dom James concocted the post of Keeper of Wayside Shrines.)

In Dom James's view, beneath Merton's restlessness and insecurity was a childhood impoverished by the absence of a sturdy, affectionate, devout Catho-

*"I find myself traveling toward my destiny in the belly of a paradox."*

(The Sign of Jonas)

lic family. Yet his immense respect for Merton was indicated by the fact that he not only encouraged Merton in his vocation as a writer but gave him key pastoral posts in community life. Merton also served as Dom James's confessor.

The Abbot met a compelling need of Merton's. Hating to say no himself, Merton depended on Dom James to say no for him, complaining all the while in his journal, but then, sooner or later, expressing relief and gratitude. Dom James served as Merton's brakes, protecting him from an impulsiveness that would have destroyed his vocation. While Merton often chafed under the Abbot's over-protectiveness, what troubled him most was his need for an over-protective abbot.

The work load Merton carried was both his own doing and Dom James's. As the end of 1949 approached, Merton felt exhausted. "I am a contemplative who is ready to collapse from overwork," he recorded in his journal on December 20:

> This, I think, is a sin and the punishment of sin, but now I have got to turn it to good use and be a saint by it, somehow. . . . The other day while the new high altar was being consecrated I found myself being stripped of one illusion after another. There I stood and sat with my eyes closed and wondered why I read so much, why I write so much, why I talk so much, and why I get so excited about things that only affect the surface of my life—I came here eight years ago and already knew better when I arrived.[186]

One factor in his exhaustion was a new responsibility in community life. Recognizing that Merton's talents as a writer equipped him for the classroom, in December 1949 Dom James assigned him to give orientation and introductory theology classes to the novices. It was the beginning of sixteen years of

teaching within the abbey community, a duty that required much of Merton's time and energy, though it had its rewards for him as well as for those he taught. Merton commented that he had learned more theology in three months of teaching than in four years of study.[187]

Exhaustion was followed by sickness. The last days of Lent in 1950 were spent in the infirmary. In September he was sent into the hospital in Louisville, and the following month returned to the abbey with orders to rest. In November he was in the hospital for nasal surgery and treatment of colitis. In December he was restored to Gethsemani feeling revived and eager to resume writing. Within three months *The Ascent to Truth* was finished as well as *Bread in the Wilderness*, a book on the eucharist. He signed a contract for four books with Harcourt, Brace.

Dom James Fox was not only a businessman eager to make Gethsemani financially self-sufficient but an Abbot open to change and reform in abbey life. Soon after his election, he began allowing professed members of the community to make use of monas-

Below:
Abbey of Gethsemani as seen from above, around 1955. (Photograph courtesy of the Abbey of Gethsemani)

*"New buildings have to be put up, and the farm has to be completely reorganized and expanded, so that all this work has to be done in a hurry, many machines are needed. When you have a great crowd of postulants, much work, new buildings, and a small mechanized army of builders all working at high pressure, the silence is not always absolutely perfect."*

(The Sign of Jonas)

tery property beyond the enclosure: the small area to which monks were limited unless required by their work. First the yard to the east of the main house was made available as a place to walk, read, and meditate; then, in 1951, the open area was expanded to include all the property on the monastery side of the main road, a large area that included meadows, ponds, and woods, while the novices were given access to a wooded bluff beyond the east wall of the enclosure. The Abbot went a step further with Merton, permitting him to take guests walking on monastery property; the privilege was later extended to other monks.

The monks' world, with Merton at the front of the line, was expanding, and just in the nick of time because within the monastery walls "you sometimes felt like you were living in a submarine," recalls Dom John Eudes Bamberger, then a novice.[188] As the fifties got underway, there were nearly 300 jammed into buildings that had once housed 70. (But the turn-over rate among novices was high. Occasionally the departures of those who decided not to stay were dramatic, like the novice who was discovered one night smoking a cigar on his straw mattress. He left in the morning.)

In June 1951, in his tenth year at Gethsemani, Merton was aware of how much he had changed: "I have become very different from what I used to be. The man who began this journal is dead, just as the man who finished *The Seven Storey Mountain* when this journal began was also dead, and what is more the man who was the central figure in *The Seven Storey Mountain* was dead over and over. . . . *The Seven Storey Mountain* is the work of a man I never even heard of."[189]

Ending thirty-six years without a national identity, Merton became a United States citizen. The step was more than a formality. For all his criticisms of the United States, and despite irritation with a

Above:
Cover of *The Secular Journal of Thomas Merton*, published in 1959 by Farrar Straus & Giroux.

Above:
Merton (front center) with scholastics. (Photograph courtesy of the Thomas Merton Studies Center)

"baby-talk citizenship textbook" he had to read in preparation, Merton felt connected to America in a way he had never experienced with France or England. Ironically, having become a monk, he felt less estranged from the society he had walked out on. "I have come to the monastery to find my place in the world," he noted in March, "and if I fail to find this place in the world, I will be wasting my time in the monastery."[190] In the Federal Courthouse in Louisville on June 22 he discovered a reporter had turned out to witness his participation in the ritual of national bonding. "This is a peculiar world," he commented in his journal, "in which the only man in a big crowd who has to worry about reporters is a Trappist monk who has left the world." It was precisely the surprise of an unworldly monk participat-

*"The one who is going to be most fully formed by the new scholastics is the Master of the Scholastics. It is as if I were beginning all over again to be a Cistercian: but this time I am doing it without asking myself the abstract questions which are the luxury and the torment of one's monastic adolescence. For now I am a grown-up monk and have no time for anything but the essentials. The only essential is not an idea or an ideal: it is God Himself, Who cannot be found by weighing the present against the future or the past but only by sinking into the heart of the present as it is."*

(The Sign of Jonas)

ing in such a worldly ceremony that made it news; also it was a story that fit in nicely with the flag-waving climate of the fifties.

At the same time, Merton was appointed Master of Scholastics—the monks being prepared for ordination. While it was a huge step away from solitude, his engagement with the scholastics introduced him to an unexpected wilderness: "What is my new desert?" he asked. "The name of it is *compassion*. There is no wilderness so terrible, so beautiful, so arid and so fruitful as the wilderness of compassion."[191]

In October 1951 Dom James found a way to give Merton greater access to the woodland and more solitude by creating the job of Forester; his tasks included selecting trees to be cut down by the novices and organizing the planting of new trees. Access to the woods brought Merton a sense of relief and liberation. "It was as though I was in another country," he noted as 1950 began.

Armed with his new title, Merton was in the company of trees day after day exploring areas of monastery land he had never seen before. One discovery, a magnificent hill, he named Mount Carmel after the mountain where Elijah heard God not as a great noise but as a whisper and on which the order of Carmelite contemplatives was founded in the twelfth century.

"It is the finest of all the knobs," Merton wrote in his journal in January 1952. "It runs north and south behind the lake knob and from the top, which is fairly clear of trees, you can see all over this part of Kentucky—miles of woods over to the northwest." The area seemed just right for a hermitage, only hermits had no place in Trappist life. "The woods cultivate me with their silences, and all day long, even in choir and at Mass, I seem to be in the forest."[192]

Sitting on a cedar log under a tree in February 1952, gazing out at light blue hills in the distance, Merton saw his true self as a kind of sea creature dwelling in a water cavern which knows of the world of dry land only by rumor. When he got free of plans and projects — the first level of the sea with its troubled surface — then he lived in the second level, in the deep waters out of reach of storms, where there was "peace, peace, peace. . . . We pray therein, slightly waving among the fish. . . . Words, as I think, do not spring from this second level. They are only meant to drown there. The question of socialization does not concern these waters. They are nobody's property. . . . No questions whatever perturb their holy botany. Neutral territory. No man's sea. I think God meant me to write about this second level." Still deeper down Merton was aware of a third level,

Below:
Photograph of the Abbey, courtesy of the Abbey of Gethsemani.

swimming in the rich darkness which is no longer thick like water but pure, like air. Starlight, and you do not know where it is coming from. Moonlight is in this prayer, stillness, waiting for the Redeemer. . . . Everything is charged with intelligence, though all is night. There is no speculation here. There is vigilance. . . . Everything is spirit. Here God is adored, His coming is recognized, He is received as soon as He is expected and because He is expected He is received, but He has passed by sooner than He arrived, He was gone before He came. He returned forever. He never yet passed by and already He had disappeared for all eternity. He is and He is not. Everything and Nothing. Not light not dark, not high not low, not this side not that side. Forever and forever. In the wind of His passing the angels cry, "The Holy One is gone." Therefore I lie dead in the air of their wings. . . . It is a strange awakening to find the sky inside you and beneath you and above you and all around you so that your spirit is one with the sky, and all is positive night.[193]

*"A tree gives glory to God first of all by being a tree. For in being what God means it to be, it is obeying Him. It 'consents,' so to speak, to His creative love. It is expressing an idea which is in God and which is not distinct from the essence of God, and therefore a tree imitates God by being a tree."*
(New Seeds of Contemplation)

Some drawings by retarded children had made their way to Merton, many of them featuring Jonas, the prophet who had risen out of the ocean, inside the whale. Regarding them as the only real works of art he had seen since arriving at Gethsemani, Merton recognized Jonas as an icon of his true self while all that was in the way of living his real identity fully was the whale in which he was buried. "Many . . . baptized in Christ have risen from the depths without troubling to find out the difference between Jonas and whale. It is the whale we cherish. Jonas swims abandoned in the heart of the sea. . . . We must get Jonas out of the whale."[194]

# The Hermit of Times Square

*The hawk is to be studied by saints and contemplatives; because he knows his business. I wish I knew my business as well as he does his.*[195]

In the prologue to *The Sign of Jonas*, published in 1953, Merton wrote:

> The sign Jesus promised to the generation that did not understand Him was the "sign of Jonas the prophet"—that is, the sign of His own resurrection. . . . Every Christian is signed with the sign of Jonas, because we all live by the power of Christ's resurrection. But I feel that my own life is especially sealed with this great sign, which baptism and monastic profession and priestly ordination have burned into the roots of my being, because like Jonas himself I find myself travelling toward my destiny in the belly of a paradox.[196]

Gethsemani was part of the paradox. Abbey life was both a desert of compassion and a field of battle.

On the battle front, Merton found himself increasingly at odds with the ways in which the monastery was making money. One of Dom James's projects to get the monastery out of debt was the creation of Gethsemani Farms, a monk-staffed commercial venture that manufactured cheese, bacon, smoked hams, and bourbon-flavored fruitcakes. The products were sold to guests and visitors at a shop by the gate house and by mail order. Alfalfa was

Opposite:
Monk inspecting cheese manufactured at the Abbey. (Photograph courtesy of Columbia University, Butler Library)

[111]

grown on monastery land, and for a while tobacco as well. A monastic factory the monks nicknamed "Little Pittsburgh" manufactured alfalfa pellets that were fed to turkeys and race horses; among those that dined on the product was a horse that won the Kentucky Derby. The campaign to make money meant a more intensive use of the work force as well, with long hours of labor in the abbey's factories. From September through mid-December the community focused its physical energies on cheese and fruitcake production. At times Merton felt he was just one more abbey business: royalties during the first few years following publication of *The Seven Storey Mountain* certainly helped to get the monastery out of debt. In later years income to the community from Merton's writing averaged $20,000 to $30,000 a year.

Merton wasn't dead-set against monastic capitalism, but was troubled by the toxic fertilizers being used on the fields, the noise of machinery, and the sense that the monastery was imitating corporate America. There were dead birds in the fields and sick monks in the infirmary with illnesses Merton didn't think had visited the monastery in the days before crop dusting. He made his views known within the community in what must have been virtuoso displays of sign language. In time his concerns about machinery and chemicals were taken seriously, though not before much harm had been done to land, health, and community life.

"By making a vow of stability," Merton wrote in the prologue to *The Sign of Jonas*, "the monk renounces the vain hope of wandering off to find a 'perfect monastery.'" This was an ideal that Merton never achieved. The ongoing struggle between Dom James and Merton centered most often on Merton's enduring attraction to what he imagined were greener monastic pastures.

By 1952, in the midst of a censorship battle with the Abbot General over *The Sign of Jonas*, Merton

*"The solitary is necessarily a man who does what he wants to do. In fact he has nothing else to do. That is why his vocation is both dangerous and despised."*

(Thoughts in Solitude)

began to hope for permission to join the Camaldoli, an order founded in the eleventh century in a valley within the Apennines. This struck him as even better suited to his needs than the Carthusians. While each Carthusian had his own room within a Charterhouse, among the Camaldolese each monk had his own separate hermitage. It was a community of solitaries living around a church. Their only common work was liturgy and prayer. "The singular advantage of such a life," Merton wrote in *The Silent Life*, "is that it makes it possible for a pure contemplative life of real solitude and simplicity, without formalism and without rigid, inflexible prescriptions of minor detail, yet fully protected by spiritual control and by religious obedience."[197] Merton's letters to the Prior General of the Camaldoli were warmly received and his interest in joining encouraged. But such a move was possible only if Merton was dispensed from the vow of stability he had taken at Gethsemani.

Dom James opposed a dispensation. He was convinced that Merton's salvation, and the salvation of others, depended on his remaining at Gethsemani. Nor was the Abbot alone in his opposition. One of Merton's friends and advisers, biblical scholar Father Barnabas Ahern, argued that withdrawal from Gethsemani would cause scandal, stir up restlessness in others, discredit the Trappists, and even encourage critics of the contemplative life.

While Merton's views on the issue shifted from day to day, a journal entry from the fall of 1952 describes an awareness to which he kept returning:

If it were merely a question of satisfying my own desires and aspirations I would leave for Camaldoli in ten minutes. Yet it is *not* merely a question of satisfying my own desires. On the contrary; there is one thing holding me at Gethsemani. And that is the cross. Some mystery of the wisdom of God has taught me that

Above:
Paperback cover of *The Silent Life*, first published in 1957 by Farrar Straus & Giroux.

perhaps after all Gethsemani is where I belong because I do not fit in and because here my ideals are practically all frustrated.[198]

Two weeks later he wrote that he had not yet completed the communal apprenticeship that clears the way to a hermitage: "I have in no way proved myself as a cenobite [a monk living in community]. I have been beating the air."[199] In the process of beating the air Merton decided that, whatever happened in his future life as a monk, he must never become an abbot. On October 8, 1952, he made a private vow, witnessed by Dom James, never to accept the office.

In his usual way, Dom James again helped Merton take another step into solitude. A vacant tool shed had been moved to the edge of the "Petrified Forest," a field populated by rain-worn statues of saints for which there was no room in the monastery buildings. Merton was given use of the shed for certain hours each day. He named his part-time hermitage St. Anne's, after the mother of Mary. Part of the writing of *No Man Is an Island* and *Bread in the Wilderness* occurred in St. Anne's. There was a period of near tranquility in his vocation, with times of deep joy. Meanwhile, with the publication of *The Sign of Jonas* early in 1952, Merton's vocational struggle and attraction to orders stressing solitude became publicly known.

By the spring of 1955, however, his wandering itch was acute once more. His hopes returned to the Carthusians. Years later he would still remember the anguish he felt while planting loblolly pines "during my 1955 crisis."[200] Dom James responded by offering Merton everything he had been campaigning for plus the possibility of doing it without changing address. Dom James was willing to release Merton from the job of Master of Scholastics and let him live as a full-time hermit. The hermitage would be the newly-built fire tower on top of Vineyard Knob that the

Below:
Fire tower in the woods surrounding Gethsemani, which Merton considered as a possible site for a hermitage. (Photograph courtesy of the Abbey of Gethsemani)

county had erected that summer. Merton already enjoyed visiting this isolated place. He was initially elated. But the practical problem of getting back and forth to the monastery for Mass and one hot meal a day proved a formidable barrier. The fire tower was a long hike from the abbey. Merton's attempt to drive a jeep ended with his being sworn at, and not in sign language, by the community's mechanic; Merton had destroyed the radiator.

Perhaps Merton read the accident as a sign that he was going in the wrong direction. Turning his back on a fire tower, Merton proposed to the Abbot that he take over the recently vacated post of Master of Novices. For Dom James, it was an astonishing about-face, yet one he welcomed. Merton was given the job, one of the most important in the community.

Yet the issue of Merton's future was still far from settled. His appeal for permission to enter another order had made its way to the Vatican. Dom James wrote to Cardinal Montini (later Pope Paul VI), one of Merton's most appreciative readers in the hierarchy and a bishop likely to have sympathy for Merton's attraction to an order that stressed solitude. Merton, Dom James wrote Montini, was "inclined to give much weight to subjective matters" and was unaware that he was a public figure both in the community and in the world outside, nor could he evaluate the impact his leaving Gethsemani would have. "Your Excellency, before God I say to you, and I am ready to meet this decision on the Last Judgment, that I cannot see the finger of God in Father Louis's desire for change." The letter must have been convincing. Merton received neither blessing nor encouragement for a transfer.

Merton's growing interest in psychoanalysis, sparked partly by his desire to be more helpful to his novices, led to a remarkable event that year which made Merton wonder about his own mental balance. In July 1956, with Father John Eudes Bamberger,

Merton flew to St. John's University in Minnesota to take part in a two-week seminar on psychiatry and its applications to religious life. Dom James planned to join them for the second week. Leading the conference was Dr. Gregory Zilboorg, a recent convert to Catholicism, whose books were published by one of the companies also tied to Merton.

Zilboorg came to their meeting loaded with preconceptions about Merton largely based on reading *The Sign of Jonas*. At a private meeting, Zilboorg told Merton that he was in "bad shape," a "semi-psychotic quack" as well as a gadfly to his superiors, to whom he kept returning until he got what he wanted.[201] His attraction to fame revealed megalomania and narcissism. He was the kind of "promoter type" who makes a killing on Wall Street one day and loses it on the horses the day after. His writing was becoming "verbological" while his "hermit trend" was pathological. As Merton listened, he couldn't help but think how much Zilboorg resembled Stalin. Yet Zilboorg was saying nothing worse than what Merton had written in his journal in his darker moments.

The next day, with Dom James's arrival, Zilboorg arranged a meeting involving both the Abbot and Merton at which Zilboorg declared that Merton's desire for greater solitude was of a piece with his longing for public attention. He wants a hermitage on Times Square "with a large sign over it saying 'HERMIT.'" This was too much for Merton. He was both humiliated and devastated. He sat in the room with tears running down his face muttering, "Stalin, Stalin." Dom James's misgivings about Merton, and Merton's about himself, had been confirmed by a famous psychiatrist.

Plans were made for Merton to come to New York for psychoanalysis with Zilboorg, but these were replaced by plans for him to see a psychologist in Louisville, Dr. James Wygal. When Zilboorg came to the abbey in December, it turned out he was having second thoughts about Merton. His condition wasn't that bad after all. "Though it transpires that I am crazy as a loon," Merton wrote Naomi Burton at the end of the year, "it turns out that I don't need analysis." In his journal a few months later, he noted that, while there were elements of insight in Zilboorg's analysis,[202] his soul could never fit into Zilboorg's "theater." To have attempted it would have been a "tragedy and a mess."[203]

In 1956, while blacks in Montgomery were boycotting segregated buses and the name of Martin

*"I dreamt I was lost in a great city and was walking 'toward the center' without quite knowing where I was going. Suddenly I came to a dead end, but on a height, looking at a great bay, an arm of the harbor. I saw a whole section of the city spread out before me on hills covered with light snow, and realized that, though I had far to go, I knew where I was: because in this city there are two arms of the harbor and they help you to find your way, as you are always encountering them."*

(Conjectures of a Guilty Bystander)

Luther King, Jr., was just beginning to be set in headline type, Merton was reading Gandhi. It was an interest that dated back to student days at Oakham though there was more to it now than taking a radical stand among classmates. It was now part of a process of exploring the social implications of the gospel as well as one of the early steps of connection with non-Christian contemplatives.

That spring also marked the beginning of Merton's immersion in Russian literature and religious writing. It was a timely interest; that fall the first Sputnik was launched. But for Merton what the Russians had to offer wasn't space travel but a profound spiritual tradition. He became convinced that restoring oneness in the church began with a recovery of oneness within oneself. A journal entry made in April 1957 eventually became part of *Conjectures of a Guilty Bystander*:

> If I can unite *in myself* the thought and the devotion of Eastern and Western Christendom, the Greek and the Latin Fathers, the Russian with the Spanish mystics, I can prepare in myself the reunion of divided Christians. From that secret and unspoken unity in myself can eventually come a visible and manifest unity of all Christians. If we want to bring together what is divided, we can not do so by imposing one division upon the other. If we do this, the union is not Christian. It is political and doomed to further conflict. We must contain all the divided worlds in ourselves and transcend them in Christ.[204]

Exploring Russian writers, Merton was among the first in the West to read Boris Pasternak's novel *Doctor Zhivago*. Astonished by the "striking and genuinely Christian elements" that marked Pasternak's writing, Merton wrote to Pasternak in August 1958 — two months before the Nobel Committee

*"I must look for my identity, somehow, not only in God but in other men.*

*I will never be able to find myself if I isolate myself from the rest of mankind as if I were a different kind of being."*

(New Seeds of Contemplation)

[118]

announced the Literature Prize would go to Pasternak:

> Although we are separated by great distances and even greater barriers, it gives me pleasure to speak to you as one with whom I feel to be a kindred spirit. It is as if we met on a deeper level of life in which individuals are not separate beings. In the language familiar to me as a Catholic monk, it is as if we were known to one another in God. This is a very simple and to me obvious expression for something quite normal and ordinary. . . . I am convinced that you understand me perfectly. It is true that a person always remains a person and utterly separate and apart from every other person. But it is equally true that each person is destined to reach with others an understanding and a unity which transcend individuality. Russian tradition describes this with a concept we do not fully possess in the west—*obornost* [conciliarity; unity in the Holy Spirit].

Merton told Pasternak that he was planning to study Russian "in order to try to get into Russian literature in the original. . . . I would much prefer to read you in Russian."

Miraculously the letter reached Pasternak's *dacha* at Peredelkino, just outside of Moscow. A response was delivered to Gethsemani in early November. Six letters were exchanged before Pasternak's death in May 1960. It was a startling experience for Merton of a oneness that cut across the artificial frontiers of politics and of ecclesiastical division. Shortly after his expulsion from the Soviet Writers Union, Pasternak told John Harris that Merton's "high feelings and prayers have saved my life."[205]

Above:
(Photograph by Naomi Burton Stone)

# Waking from a Dream

*The Christian life ... is a continual discovery of Christ in new and unexpected places.*

In one of Merton's letters to Boris Pasternak he confided a dream that he had experienced in February 1958. He dreamt he was "sitting with a very young Jewish girl of fourteen or fifteen, and that she suddenly manifested a very deep and pure affection for me and embraced me so that I was moved to the depths of my soul. I learned that her name was 'Proverb,' which I thought very simple and beautiful. And also I thought: 'She is of the race of Saint Anne.' I spoke to her of her name, and she did not seem to be proud of it, because it seemed that the other young girls mocked her for it. But I told her that it was a very beautiful name, and there the dream ended. . . . Thus you are initiated into the scandalous secret of a monk who is in love with a girl, and a Jew at that! One cannot expect much from monks these days. The heroic asceticism of the past is no more."

The dream was connected in his mind, Merton continued, to an experience that occurred several weeks later, on March 18. He was in Louisville on an editorial errand, "walking alone in the crowded street and suddenly saw that everybody was Proverb and that in all of them shone her extraordinary beauty and purity and shyness, even though they did not know who they were and were perhaps ashamed of their names because they were mocked on account of them. And they did not know their real identity as the Child so dear to God who, from

Opposite:
Merton writing in a tool shed on the Abbey grounds. (Photograph courtesy of Columbia University, Butler Library)

*"Writing is the one thing that gives me access to some real silence and solitude. Also I find that it helps me to pray, because when I pause at my work I find that the mirror inside me is surprisingly clean and deep and serene and God shines there and is immediately found, without hunting, as if He had come close to me while I was writing."*

(The Sign of Jonas)

before the beginning, was playing in His sight all days, playing in the world."[206]

The experience Merton shared with Pasternak was first recorded in his journal the day after it occurred. In a text built on the journal entry, it became part of *Conjectures of a Guilty Bystander*:

In Louisville, at the corner of Fourth and Walnut, in the center of the shopping district, I was suddenly overwhelmed with the realization that I loved all those people, that they were mine and I theirs, that we could not be alien to one another even though we were total strangers. It was like waking from a dream of separateness, of spurious self-isolation in a special world, the world of renunciation and supposed holiness. The whole illusion of a separate holy existence is a dream. . . . This sense of liberation from an illusory difference was such a relief and such a joy to me that I almost laughed out loud. . . . It is a glorious destiny to be a member of the human race, though it is a race dedicated to many absurdities and one which makes many terrible mistakes: yet, with all that, God Himself gloried in becoming a member of the human race. A member of the human race! To think that such a commonplace realization should suddenly seem like news that one holds the winning ticket in a cosmic sweepstake. . . . There is no way of telling people that they are all walking around shining like the sun. . . . There are no strangers! . . . If only we could see each other [as we really are] all the time. There would be no more war, no more hatred, no more cruelty, no more greed. . . . I suppose the big problem would be that we would fall down and worship each other. . . . The gate of heaven is everywhere.[207]

*"When I wrote this book the fact uppermost in my mind was that I had seceded from the world of my time in all clarity and with total freedom . . . Since that time, I have learned, I believe, to look back into that world with greater compassion, seeing those in it not as alien to myself, not as peculiar and deluded strangers, but as identified with myself . . . [T]he monastery is not an 'escape' from the world. On the contrary, by being in the monastery I take my true part in all the struggles and sufferings of the world."*
(Preface to the Japanese edition of The Seven Storey Mountain)

One of the main surprises in Merton's life, astonishing at least as much to him as to those who came to

[122]

know him through his early books, was the connection that Merton made with the world during the latter part of his monastic life. On the one hand he was being drawn toward solitude, and on the other ever more deeply into engagement with people and events distant from the monastery.

At Fourth and Walnut in 1958 Merton discovered one of the main illusions that had survived his first seventeen years of monastic life: the idea that sanctity required radical separation within "the world of renunciation and supposed holiness." The experience did not suggest to him that he ought to give up his monastic vocation or his aspiration to become a hermit, but his understanding of what it meant to be a monk was transformed: authentic solitude must be a place both of nonpresence and attendance, nonparticipation and engagement, hiddenness and hospitality, disappearance and arrival. The opposites need each other as birds need two wings.

In editing *The Hidden Ground of Love*, Msgr. William Shannon, general editor of the Merton letters, noticed that Merton's correspondence "took off after the event at Fourth and Walnut."[208] Merton began opening more and more lines of contact and dialogue with people beyond the monastery.

One of the people to whom he started writing was Dorothy Day, founder of the Catholic Worker movement. He had met her when she came to speak at St. Bonaventure's when he was teaching there, but there had been no further contact between them. If Merton at the time was the main symbol of Catholic withdrawal from the world, this often-jailed woman was the main representative of Catholic immersion in the world. She edited *The Catholic Worker*, an independent, lay-edited journal which was the only pacifist publication within the Catholic Church. The houses of hospitality associated with the Catholic Worker were in the most impoverished urban neighborhoods. Her criticisms of an economic system that produced such a multitude of destitute,

Below:
Dorothy Day, founder of the Catholic Worker movement. (Photograph courtesy of Maryknoll archives)

damaged, and abandoned people led many Catholics to consider her a Communist, though for others, like Merton, she was one of the rare individuals living the gospel without compromise, much as Saint Francis of Assisi had done. Merton expressed his appreciation in a letter sent in July 1959:

> I am touched deeply by your witness for peace [her recent arrest in City Hall Park, New York, for refusing to take shelter during air raid drills]. You are very right in going at it along the lines of *Satyagraha* [literally "truth-force," Gandhi's word for nonviolence]. I see no other way, though of course the angles of the problem are not all clear. I am certainly with you on taking some kind of stand and acting accordingly. Nowadays it is no longer a question of who is right, but who is at least not criminal, if any of us can say that anymore. So don't worry about whether or not in every point you are perfectly all right according to everybody's book; you are right before God as far as you can go and you are fighting for a truth that is clear enough and important enough. What more can anybody do? ... It was never more true than now that the world is lost and cannot see true values. Let us keep on praying for one another.[209]

*"It is my intention to make my entire life a rejection of, a protest against the crimes and injustices of war and political tyranny which threaten to destroy the whole race of man and the world with him. By my monastic life and vows I am saying NO to all the concentration camps, the aerial bombardments, the staged political trials, the judicial murders, the racial injustices, [etc.] ... If I say NO to all these secular forces, I also say YES to all that is good in the world and in man."*

(Introductions East and West)

Such prayers were urgently sought. At the time Merton was struggling with a desire not only for greater solitude but to live his monastic life in a situation of real poverty of the sort embraced by Dorothy Day. He found Gethsemani, with its fine buildings and expensive machinery, too much a fixture of a wealthy, militaristic nation. A Benedictine abbot in Mexico had invited Merton to establish a hermitage near his monastery; the Bishop of San Juan offered him a hermitage on the island of Tortola in the British West Indies. And there was an invitation

from the poet Ernesto Cardenal, a former novice at
Gethsemani, to be part of an experimental monastic
community in Nicaragua. Merton again asked his superiors, within the order and in Rome, if it might not be
God's will for him to make such a move.

In mid-November Dom James left hurriedly for
Rome to argue the case for Merton remaining at
Gethsemani. Even then Merton found himself looking at Gethsemani with the eyes of someone about
to leave. While in Louisville he stopped at a travel
agency to find out about tickets to Latin America.

On December 17 a letter from Rome reached him
which he read on his knees before the Blessed Sacrament in the novitiate chapel. Cardinals Larraona
and Valeri, of the Vatican's Sacred Congregation for
Religious, quoted a passage from Merton's *No Man
Is an Island* in which Merton affirmed his Trappist
vocation, not because it was the best vocation, but
because it was "the one God has willed for me."[210]
(Ironically, the quotation in the letter broke off
before reaching that part of the original text in
which Merton wrote that, if God willed something
else for him, he "would turn to it on the instant.")
The cardinals spoke of the scandal that would be
caused were Merton to leave Gethsemani.

While the Vatican letter was not the answer he
had hoped and prayed for, the cardinals' refusal to
provide a *transitus* was a relief. Merton went for a
walk. "Coming back, [I] walked around a corner of
the woods and the monastery swung into view. I
burst out laughing. It was no longer the same place,
no longer heavy. I was free from it."[211]

Two days later he presented Dom James with
both a statement of submission and a declaration
concerning rights of conscience. Merton stated that
he would "take no further positive steps" to leave
the order and "will apply no pressure to do so" apart
from "manifesting my thoughts to Superiors or those
who are competent." He reminded Dom James that
every monk is free to receive advice from spiritual

directors of his own choosing. "Do you not tend to assume that your policies represent the last word in the spiritual perfection of every one of your subjects, and that anyone who is drawn to another way is leaving the path of perfection? ... I appeal to the right ... to consult directors outside the monastery by letter without interference, so that this problem of mine can be settled. I am only asking for things which the Church wishes her subjects to have, not for anything unreasonable."[212]

Increasingly Merton was distressed by the lack of respect for conscience and freedom within his order and within the church. Dom James was blocking letters to Merton from Cardenal despite Merton's appeal that the correspondence involved matters of conscience. Struggles with censors and superiors over his writings persisted as did his irritation with his abbey and Abbot.

During the latter half of the year, apart from keeping the journal, his writing was nearly at a halt. His main book work was revising and editing *Disputed Questions*, which included his Pasternak essay as well as writings about Eastern Orthodoxy and desert monasticism, and *The New Man*, which centered on the search for the true self, made in the image and likeness of God, that is hidden beneath name, title, achievements, and illusions.

As 1959 drew to a close, Merton decided, with Dom James's blessing, that it was time to begin psychoanalysis with Dr. James Wygal in Louisville. The idea had originally come up at the time Gregory Zilboorg labeled Merton the Hermit of Times Square. It wasn't that Merton was worried about pathological impulses threatening his sanity, but it would be good to have a trained, detached, and caring listener to help him see himself and those around him in fresh perspective. It proved helpful. While it seems very little psychoanalysis occurred in the years that followed, Jim Wygal helped Merton cope with his stress. At the same time a friendship was founded that lasted the rest of Merton's life.

# Blessings

*God . . . does not need to keep the birds in cages.*

As 1960 began, it was clear that a hermitage somewhere else was out of the question. Merton's hopes focused on a hermitage at Gethsemani. In conversations with Dom James the idea developed for a house out of sight of the monastery buildings that could function both as an ecumenical conference center and also serve as a place of part-time seclusion for Merton.

On March 31 Merton was given a quiet cell within the monastery. Its one window gave a wonderful view of Rohan's Knob and Holy Cross. This was, Merton wrote in his journal, "a nice hermitage." Early in May, still rejoicing, he wrote about the sense he had while in his tiny cell of sitting "on the edge of the sky." He had a stool, his old scriptorium desk, a bed, three icons, and a small crucifix made by Ernesto Cardenal. "Reading in here is a totally different experience from anywhere else, as if the silence of the four walls enriched everything with great significance. One is alone, not on guard, utterly relaxed and receptive. Having four walls and silence all around enables you to listen . . . with all the pores of your skin and to absorb the truth through every part of your being. I doubt if I would be any better off in Mexico!"[213]

Another sign of new curtains rising was direct contact with the Pope. It was something that Merton had hoped for in 1958, when, a few weeks after the election of John XXIII, Merton wrote him a letter describ-

Below:
Pope John XXIII, who convened the Second Vatican Council. Merton sensed in Pope John a new spirit of openness to the world. (Photograph courtesy of Maryknoll archives)

*"For many people he has restored hope in the Church as a living reality, as the true Body of Christ. He has made the reality of the Spirit in the world once more simply and profoundly credible even to people who are not easily disposed to believe in anything."*
(Conjectures of a Guilty Bystander)

ing his vision of a monastery, perhaps in Latin America, where special groups—especially writers and intellectuals—might come for retreats and discussions.[214]

Fourteen months later, on February 11, 1960, Merton received a packet from the Vatican that contained a portrait photograph signed by John as well as a blessing for the novitiate. Responding the same day, Merton told John that he had received permission "to start, very discreetly, a small retreat project" aimed at Protestant and Catholic theologians, psychiatrists, writers, and artists—something on the lines he had described in his previous letter to John but at Gethsemani rather than in Latin America. "Our goal," Merton wrote, "is to bring together . . . various groups of people highly qualified in their own field who are interested in the spiritual life, no matter what aspect, and who will be able to profit from an informal contact, from a spiritual and cultural dialogue, with Catholic contemplatives."[215]

A nonverbal reply reached Gethsemani on April 11 with the arrival of Lorenzo Barbato, a Venetian architect who was a personal friend of the pontiff's. Barbato brought Merton a liturgical vestment, a stole, which had been used by Pope John XXIII. John wanted Merton to have it. Totally unexpected, the present was a startling indication of John's affection and respect for Merton.[216]

In Barbato's care, Merton sent the Pope a copy of his latest book, *The Wisdom of the Desert*, a collection of sayings and stories of the Desert Fathers, wilderness hermits from the early church who were especially dear to Merton. In an accompanying letter Merton told John of the progress being made with the ecumenical project. "A few days ago I had the pleasure of addressing more than fifty Protestant seminarians and pastors here in our monastery. They showed remarkable good will. . . . I spoke to them . . . as a brother." (Thirty years later it is hard to remember the frigid climate that then existed between Catholics and Prot-

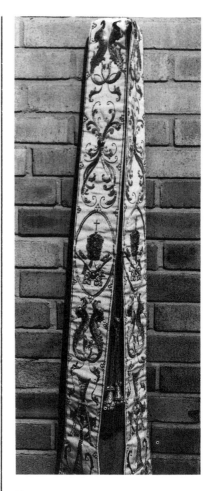

Above:
The stole worn by Pope John XXIII at his coronation, presented to Merton as a gift. (Photograph courtesy of the Abbey of Gethsemani)

*"How can I express to you my gratitude and the emotion with which I received the honor bestowed on me by Your Holiness in sending me this beautiful stole, worn and blessed by Your Holiness. It is truly the greatest honor of my life . . ."*

(Letter to Pope John XXIII, April 11, 1960)

estants and how astonishing such dialogue was.)
Aware of John's special interest in the Orthodox
Church, Merton went on to mention his contact with
an Orthodox priest in Paris.

Two weeks later Dom James received a letter from
Cardinal Tardini, the Vatican Secretary of State,
expressing the particular interest Pope John had in the
"retreats with Protestants which Father Louis was
organizing at Our Lady of Gethsemani." Plans for the
Second Vatican Council had been announced in 1959
and Pope John had decided Protestant and Orthodox
Christians would also have a place in the event. The
ecumenical dialogues Merton was initiating at Gethsemani couldn't be more timely.

In late April Merton suggested a skete (a small
monastic household) be built on Mount Olivet, a
crest behind the sheep barn, not quite a mile from
the abbey, in range of its bells. Dom James gave his
approval. On May 18 Merton marked the trees to be
cut down to make room for the "Mount Olivet
Retreat Center." In October, when the contractor
arrived to stake out the building site, Merton was
referring to the place not as a conference center but,
"let's be frank, the hermitage."[217]

By the end of the month, with construction
underway, the cinderblock building had its real
name, after the patroness of his vocation: the hermitage of Saint Mary of Carmel. Mary was "this
queen of mine to the end of the ages."[218]

Merton lit the first blaze in the fireplace December 2. Eleven days later, on the nineteenth anniversary of his reception as a postulant, Merton took
possession of the hermitage, though Dom James only
permitted him use of it a few hours each day. "Lit
candles in the dusk," he wrote joyfully in his journal
December 26. "The sense of a journey ended, of
wandering at an end. The first time in my life I ever
really felt that I had come home and that my roam-
ing and looking were ended."

*"My dear Holy Father,*
*. . . It seems to me that, as a contemplative,*
*I do not need to lock myself into solitude and*
*lose all contact with the rest of the world; rather,*
*this poor world has a right to my solitude . . . "*
*(Letter to Pope John XXIII,*
*November 10, 1958)*

# Hagia Sophia

*. . . as if the Blessed Virgin herself, as if Wisdom, had awakened me.*

As 1961 began, Merton was home at last, if only part time. During reading periods at the hermitage, he immersed himself in the writings of mystics. His love of the fourteenth-century English recluse Saint Julian of Norwich dates from this period. Supplanting even Saint John of the Cross in his affections, he saw her as "without doubt one of the most wonderful of all Christian voices."[219] Julian, writing of "Jesus our Mother" and "Mother Jesus," helped to open the door to Merton's exploration of God's feminine aspect and at the same time to link his dream of Proverb with Holy Wisdom.

For several years Merton had been thinking about *Hagia Sophia*—Holy Wisdom. The Greek phrase had entered his mind in 1957 while reading Russian mystics who were fascinated with those passages in the Book of Proverbs in which "Wisdom is 'playing in the world' before the face of the Creator." He noted in his journal that the church identified *Hagia Sophia* as being revealed and fulfilled both in Mary and in the church.[220]

In 1958 Merton had written Boris Pasternak about his dream of Proverb, the Jewish girl whose passionate but virginal embrace had moved him so deeply. It was an encounter, he realized, with *Hagia Sophia*. The dream so impressed him that a few days later he wrote Proverb a letter expressing gratitude for her loving in him "something which I thought I

Opposite:
Merton at work in his hermitage. (Photograph by John Howard Griffin)

*"One might say I had decided to marry the silence of the forest. The sweet dark warmth of the whole world will have to be my wife."*
("Day of a Stranger")

had entirely lost, and someone who, I thought, had long ago ceased to be. . . . I love your name, its mystery, its simplicity, and its secret."[221] Two weeks later he wrote to her again, assuring her that he was keeping his promise not to speak of her until he saw her again, as he felt he had the day before, March 18, among the people at Fourth and Walnut in Louisville. "I shall never forget our meeting yesterday. The touch of your hand makes me a different person. To be with you is rest and Truth. Only with you are all things found, dear child, sent by God."[222]

He glimpsed her again in a painting by Victor Hammer when he was visiting the Hammer household in Lexington, Kentucky, in April 1959. As in his dream, she was a young Semitic woman. She represented Mary, Hammer explained. In the painting she was placing a crown on Christ's head. In May, writing Hammer about the blaze the painting had lit within him, Merton commented, "The feminine principle in the universe is the inexhaustible source of creative realization of [God's] glory."[223]

July 2, 1960, the Feast of Our Lady's Visitation, when Merton was in the hospital in Louisville for X-rays, he had a Proverb-like dream in which he was awakened by "the soft voice of the nurse. . . . It was like awakening for the first time from all the dreams of life — as if the Blessed Virgin herself, as if Wisdom, had awakened me."[224] The gentle voice he had heard in his dream was, he knew, the voice of *Hagia Sophia.*

Visiting a Cincinnati museum in October to gather prints for the novitiate and his hermitage, he thought he had met Proverb in the flesh when he encountered "a Jewish girl sitting on top of the filing cabinets with her shoes off."[225]

Little by little Merton's prose poem, *Hagia Sophia,* was taking shape.

"There is in all visible things," the completed work began, "an invisible fecundity, a dimmed light, a meek namelessness, a hidden wholeness. This mys-

*"She is in all things like the air receiving the sunlight. In her they prosper. In her they glorify God. In her they rejoice to reflect Him. In her they are united with Him. She is the union between them. She is the love that unites them. She is life as communion, life as thanksgiving, life as praise, life as festival, life as glory."*
("Hagia Sophia")

terious Unity and Integrity is Wisdom, the Mother of all, *Natura naturans*.[226] There is in all things an inexhaustible sweetness and purity, a silence that is a fount of action and joy. It rises up in wordless gentleness and flows out to me from the unseen roots of all created being, welcoming me tenderly."[227]

He described himself waking in the hospital, at once all mankind and, at the same time, Adam, while she who is waking him was not only Eve but Mary and the feminine child playing before the Creator. She was the union between Creator and creation, God not only as Father but Mother, the Divine nature, the mercy and tenderness of God, the Wisdom of God: *Hagia Sophia*.

The poem was a celebration of the discovery of the feminine dimension of God. Appropriately, Victor Hammer was the first to publish *Hagia Sophia*, producing an exquisite handprinted edition set in American Uncial, a typeface of his own design inspired by medieval monastic calligraphy.

Other writings from the period reveal the political side of Merton running side-by-side with the mystical.

In "A Signed Confession of Crimes Committed Against the State," Merton admits he is "sitting under a pine tree doing absolutely nothing," has done nothing for an hour, and intends to continue doing nothing. "I confess that I have been listening to a mockingbird. Yes, I admit that it is a mockingbird. . . . Clearly I am not worthy to exist another minute."[228]

Reading William Shirer's *The Rise and Fall of the Third Reich* inspired the writing of "Chant to Be Used Around a Site With Furnaces," a chilling poem in monotone voice about the administration of the Holocaust, in which improvement equals more efficient methods of death and those who try to save lives are the guilty ones. "All the while I obeyed perfectly," says the narrator-commander who, before his execution for war crimes, was a man of self-sacri-

Above:
Paperback cover of *The New Man*, first published in 1961 by Farrar Straus & Giroux.

*"The sanity of Eichmann is disturbing . . . We can no longer assume that because a man is 'sane' he is therefore in his 'right mind.' The whole concept of sanity in a society where spiritual values have lost their meaning is itself meaningless."*
("A Devout Meditation in Memory of Adolf Eichmann")

fice whose work was conscientious and faultless; he stands not only for Hitler's Holocaust but for the nuclear holocaust being prepared by those who defeated the Nazis. "Do not think yourself better because you burn up friends and enemies with long-range missiles without ever seeing what you have done."[229] In the year of the United States-sponsored Bay of Pigs Invasion of Cuba and the Soviet-backed erection of the Berlin Wall, a future nuclear holocaust seemed increasingly likely.

In the same period Merton wrote "Original Child Bomb," the title being an exact translation of the Japanese word for the bomb that had been dropped on Hiroshima on August 6, 1945.[230]

The poem was a short history written in numbered, laconic sentences about the development and first use of nuclear weapons, despite the appeal of some of the bomb's makers that it not be used without prior warning. Nonetheless, the bomb was dropped on a city considered of minor military importance. "The people who were near the center became nothing. The whole city was blown to bits and the ruins caught fire instantly everywhere, burning briskly. 70,000 people were killed right away or died within a few hours. Those who did not die at once suffered great pain. Few of them were soldiers." Merton noted the odd way that religious terms had been used by those associated with the bomb. Its first test was called Trinity. The mission to drop the Hiroshima bomb returned to Papacy, the code name for Tinian.

In the midst of some of his best writing, Merton was full of doubts about his work. "I become more and more skeptical about my writing," he told Dorothy Day. "There has been some good and much bad, and I haven't been nearly honest enough and clear enough. The problem that torments me is that I can so easily become part of a general system of delusion. . . . I find myself more and more drifting toward the derided and possibly quite absurd and

Below:
Survivor of atomic blast at Nagasaki. (Photograph by Yosuke Yamahata/United Nations, courtesy of Maryknoll archives)

*"As to the Original Child that was now born, President Truman summed up the philosophy of the situation in a few words. 'We found the bomb,' he said, 'and we used it.'"*
("Original Child Bomb")

defeatist position of a sort of Christian anarchist."[231]

Always gifted to find bonding words with those to whom he was communicating, "anarchist" to Dorothy Day meant someone like herself: a person whose obedience was not to rulers, states, or systems but to the gospel. In a letter written a few weeks later, he said, "I don't feel that I can in conscience, at a time like this, go on writing just about things like meditation, though that has its point. I cannot just bury my head in a lot of rather tiny and secondary monastic studies either. I think I have to face the big issues, the life-and-death issues: and this is what everyone is afraid of."[232]

In September 1961 Merton was ready to go public about his thinking on war, doing so with "The Root of War Is Fear," an essay that had once been a short chapter in *Seeds of Contemplation*, and which he had revised and expanded for the forthcoming *New Seeds of Contemplation*. But the version he sent to Dorothy Day included several paragraphs written especially for *The Catholic Worker*:

The present war crisis is something we have made entirely for and by ourselves. There is in reality not the slightest logical reason for war, and yet the whole world is plunging headlong into frightful destruction, and doing so with the purpose of avoiding war. . . . This is true war-madness, an illness of the mind and spirit that is spreading with a furious and subtle contagion all over the world. Of all the countries that are sick, America is perhaps the most grievously afflicted. On all sides we have people building bomb shelters where, in case of nuclear war, they will simply bake slowly instead of burning quickly or being blown out of existence in a flash. And they are prepared to sit in these shelters with machine guns with which to prevent their neighbor from entering. This in a nation that claims to be fighting for religious truth along with freedom and other values of the spirit. Truly we have entered the "post-Christian era" with a vengeance. Whether we are destroyed or whether we survive, the future is awful to contemplate.

What is the place of the Christian in all this? Is he simply to fold his hands and resign himself for the worst, accepting it as the inescapable will of God and preparing himself to enter heaven with a sigh of relief? Should he open up the Apocalypse and run into the street to give everyone his idea of what is happening? Or, worse still should he take a hard-headed and "practical" attitude about it and join in the madness of the war makers, calculating how, by a "first strike," the glorious Christian West can eliminate atheistic communism for all time and usher in the millennium? I am no prophet and seer but it seems to me that this last position may very well be the most diabolical of illusions, the great and not even subtle temptation

Below:
Partial front page of the October 1961 issue of *The Catholic Worker*, which featured "The Root of War," Merton's first contribution to the pacifist newspaper.

# THE CATHOLIC WORKER

Vol. XXVIII  No. 3                    October, 1961            Subscription: 25c Per Year            Price 1c

## THE WORKER PRIESTS

### By Anne Taillefer

"Man is a living paradox and the Incarnation—the Word made flesh—is the greatest paradox of all" (Henri de Lubac). Thus vocation, the call of the supernatural to the natural, the message of the Lord, when utterly pure and obediently heard is apt to surprise us shatteringly. Of all the strange vocations that of worker-priest may be among the most dispossessed.

The present Anglican bishop of Tanganyika, who was then Father Trevor Huddleston, one of the great fighters against apartheid in South Africa, once said: "the trial of the worker-priests is that of Joan of Arc". Strangely enough his words are echoed in a letter written by an eminent ecclesiastic, years ago, to Father Godin, one of the founders of the movement. "It is doubtful if the Catholic Church, the Catholic hierarchy, by itself would have the courage to operate this reform.

## THE ROOT OF WAR

### By Thomas Merton

The present war crisis is something we have made entirely for and by ourselves. There is in reality not the slightest logical reason for war, and yet the whole world is plunging headlong into frightful destruction, and doing so **with the purpose of avoiding war and preserving peace!** This is a true war-madness, an illness of the mind and the spirit that is spreading with a furious and subtle contagion all over the world. Of all the countries that are sick, America is perhaps the most grievously afflicted. On all sides we have people building bomb shelters where, in case of nuclear war, they will simply bake slowly instead of burning up quickly or being blown out of existence in a flash. And they are prepared to sit in these shelters with machine guns with which to prevent their neighbor from entering. This in a nation that claims to be fighting for religious truth along with freedom of a Christianity that has grown rich and comfortable, and is satisfied with its riches.

What are we to do? The duty of the Christian in this crisis is to strive with all his power and intelligence, with his faith, his hope in Christ, and love for God and man, to do the one task which God has imposed upon us in the world today. That task is to work for the total abolition of war. There can be no question that unless war is abolished the world will remain constantly in a state of madness and desperation in which, because of the immense destructive power of modern weapons, the danger of catastrophe will be imminent and probable at every moment everywhere. Unless we set ourselves immediately to this task, both as individuals and in our political and religious groups, we tend by our very passivity and fatalism to cooperate with the destructive forces that are leading inexorably to war. It is a problem of terrifying complexity and magnitude, for which the Church itself is not fully able to see clear and decisive solutions. Yet she must lead the way on the road to the nonviolent settlement of difficulties and toward the gradual abolition of war as the way of settling international or civil disputes. Christians must become active in every possible way, mobilizing all their resources for the fight against war.

First of all there is much to be learned. Peace is to be preached, nonviolence is to be explained as a practical method, and not left to be mocked as an outlet for crackpots who want to make a show of themselves. Prayer and sacrifice must be used as the most effective spiritual weapons in the war against war, and like all weapons, they must be used with deliberate aim: not just with a vague aspiration for peace and security, but against violence and war. This implies that we are also willing to sacrifice and

*"As for writing: I don't feel that I can in conscience, at a time like this, go on writing just about things like meditation, though that has its point. I cannot just bury my head in a lot of rather tiny and secondary monastic studies either. I think I have to face the big issues, the life-and-death issues: and this is what everyone is afraid of."*
(*Letter to Dorothy Day, August 23, 1961*)

[137]

restrain our own instinct for violence and aggressiveness in our relations with other people. We may never succeed in this campaign but whether we succeed or not, the duty is evident.[233]

Merton was aware that many who treasured *The Seven Storey Mountain* would be troubled, some irate, at a line of thinking so critical of what America was doing. With John F. Kennedy's inauguration in January 1961, the United States government was led by a Catholic who enjoyed overwhelming Catholic support; quite apart from this, US policy traditionally had the determined support of the American Catholic population and hierarchy. On October 23, shortly after the essay was published, he wrote in his journal:

I am perhaps at the turning point in my spiritual life, perhaps slowly coming to a point of maturation and the resolution of doubts — and the forgetting of fears. Walking into a known and definite battle. May God protect me in it. *The Catholic Worker* sent out a press release about my article, which may have many reactions. . . . I am one of the few Catholic priests in the country who has come out unequivocally for a completely intransigent fight for the abolition of war and the use of nonviolent means to settle international conflicts. Hence by implication not only against the bomb, against nuclear testing, against Polaris submarines, but against all violence. This I will inevitably have to explain in due course. Nonviolent action, not mere passivity. How am I going to explain myself and defend a definite position in a timely manner when it takes at least two months to get even a short article through the censors of the Order, is a question I cannot attempt to answer.

# Silencing

*The monk is the one supposedly attuned to the inner spiritual dimension of things. If he hears nothing, and says nothing, then the renewal as a whole will be in danger and may be completely sterilized.*

"The Root of War Is Fear" was followed quickly by more essays on the same theme in *The Catholic Worker* and other publications. One of them was *Fellowship*, the magazine of the ecumenical pacifist organization, the Fellowship of Reconciliation. Merton joined the FOR in November 1961, signing a statement of purpose that included the pledge not to fight in war or assist in any way in preparations for combat.

In a letter to Pope John XXIII Merton voiced alarm at the way in which many Americans, due to ignorance and the influence of propaganda, linked their opposition to Communism with readiness to use the American nuclear arsenal to destroy the Soviet Union. Catholics were prominent among the most intransigent, regarding their hawkish position as a sign of loyalty to the church. The economy itself depends increasingly on preparation for war, he went on, so that disarmament is seen as an economic threat. "A very small peace movement, bringing Protestants and Catholics together [the Fellowship of Reconciliation], has come into being in the United States," he told the Pope. "I try to be a part of this movement as much as I can, here in the cloister, through my prayers and writings and

Above:
The cross that stood before Merton's hermitage. (Photograph by Jim Forest, courtesy of Boston College, Burns Library)

also through the conversations I have with those who come here."[234]

The topics Merton was writing about as 1961 came to an end were not welcomed by the Trappist's Abbot General, Dom Gabriel Sortais, nor did most of the order's censors see such controversial writing as appropriate for a monk. Late in 1961, Merton wrote to me (as one of the editors of *The Catholic Worker*) that the censorship he was encountering was "completely and deliberately obstructive, not aimed at combing out errors at all, but purely and simply at preventing the publication of material that 'doesn't look good.' And this means anything that ruffles in any way the censors' tastes or susceptibilities."[235]

Many readers besides the censors were irritated. An editorial in *The Washington Catholic Standard* in March 1962 described Merton as "an absolute pacifist" and accused him of disregarding "authoritative Catholic utterances and [making] unwarranted charges about the intention of our government towards disarmament."

As such criticism mounted, Merton was forced to withdraw his name as editor of *Breakthrough to Peace*, a book of essays on the arms race which he had conceived and assembled for New Directions, but at least the project itself was not derailed.[236]

Looking for a way to share his thinking about the religious dimension of social and political problems without having to pass through the labyrinths of censorship, Merton produced *Cold War Letters*, a book-sized mimeographed collection of recent letters; some of his correspondents were enlisted to help circulate the text. It was Merton's first experience of being read in *samizdat* (Russian for self-published), thus forging another link with Russian writers like Pasternak. Merton at least had a limited degree of support from his Abbot. Dom James assented to the circulation of Merton's writing in mimeographed form, deciding that censorship was

*"We find ourselves confronting the possibility of nuclear war with more than the common and universal urgency, because we Christians are at least dimly aware that this is a matter of choice for us and that the future of Christianity on earth may depend on the moral quality of the decision we are making."*
(Thomas Merton on Peace)

COLD WAR LETTERS:    PREFACE

These copies of letters written over a period of little more than one year pre-ceeding the Cuban Crisis of 1962, have been made for friends who might be expected to understand something of the writer's viewpoint, even when they might not agree with all he has said, still less with all that he may have unconsciously implied.

As a matter of fact, the letters themselves have been copied practically without change, except that the more irrelevant parts have been cut out. There have been none of the careful corrections, qualifications, and omissions which would be re-quired before such a book could possibly be considered for general circulation, or even for any but the most limited and private reading. As it stands, it lies open to all kinds of misinterpretation, and malevolence will not find it difficult to read into these pages the most sinister of attitudes. A few words in a preface may then serve to deny in advance the possible allegations of witch hunters.

required only for material that had the potential of reaching the general public.

Many hours were devoted to work on a book that he hoped would be moderate enough to pass inspection by the Abbot General and the censors: *Peace in the Post-Christian Era*. The manuscript had just been completed when a letter arrived ordering him to give up all such writing projects.

"Now here is the axe," he wrote to me on April 29, 1962. "For a long time I have been anticipating trouble with the higher superiors and now I have it. The orders are, no more writing about peace. ... In substance I am being silenced on the subject of war and peace."

The decision, he said, reflected "an astounding incomprehension of the seriousness of the present crisis in its religious aspect. It reflects an insensitivity to Christian and Ecclesiastical values, and to the real sense of the monastic vocation. The reason given is that this is not the right kind of work for a monk and that it 'falsifies the monastic message.' Imagine that: the thought that a monk might be deeply enough concerned with the issue of nuclear war to voice a protest against the arms race, is supposed to bring the monastic life into *disrepute*. Man, I would think that it might just possibly salvage a last shred of repute for an institution that many consider to be dead on its feet. . . . That is really the most absurd aspect of the whole situation, that these people insist on digging their own grave and erecting over it the most monumental kind of tombstone."

Beneath the surface of the disagreement between Merton and the Abbot General was a different conception of the identity and mission of the church. In his letter he stated, "The vitality of the Church depends precisely on spiritual renewal, uninterrupted, continuous, and deep. Obviously this renewal is to be expressed in the historical context, and will call for a real spiritual understanding of historical crises, an evaluation of them in terms of their inner significance and in terms of man's growth and the advancement of truth in man's world: in other words, the establishment of the 'kingdom of God.' The monk is the one supposedly attuned to the inner spiritual dimension of things. If he hears nothing, and says nothing, then the renewal as a whole will be in danger and may be completely sterilized."

Those silencing him, he went on in white heat, regarded the monk as someone appointed not to see or hear anything new but "to support the already existing viewpoints . . . defined for him by somebody else. Instead of being in the advance guard, he is in the rear with the baggage, confirming all that has been done by the officials. . . . He has no other function, then, except perhaps to pray for what he is told to pray for: namely the purposes and the objectives of an ecclesiastical bureaucracy. . . . He must in no event and under no circumstances assume a role

*"My peace writings have reached an abrupt halt. Told not to do any more on this subject. Dangerous, subversive, perilous, offensive to pious ears, and confusing to good Catholics who are all at peace in the nice idea that we ought to wipe Russia off the face of the earth. Why get people all stirred up?"*

*(Letter to Daniel Berrigan,
December 7, 1961)*

that implies any form of spontaneity and originality. He must be an eye that sees nothing except what is carefully selected for him to see. An ear that hears nothing except what it is advantageous for the managers for him to hear. We know what Christ said about such ears and eyes."

Merton asked if he shouldn't "just blast the whole thing wide open, or walk out, or tell them to jump in the lake?" Wouldn't it be justified to disobey such manifestly unjust orders? After all, as he pointed out, obedience is synonymous with love. But would disobedience or a public denunciation be seen as a witness for peace and for the truth of the church, in its reality, rather than some figment of the imagination? Wouldn't such action rather be seen by his fellow monks as an excuse for dismissing a minority viewpoint and be regarded by those outside as fresh proof that the church had no love for private conscience? Whose mind would be changed?

"In my own particular case," he concluded, public protest and disobedience "would backfire and be fruitless. It would be taken as a witness *against* the peace movement and would confirm these people in all the depth of their prejudices and their self-complacency. It would reassure them in every possible way that they are incontrovertibly right and make it even more impossible for them ever to see any kind of new light on the subject. And in any case I am not merely looking for opportunities to blast off. I can get along without it.

"I am where I am. I have freely chosen this state, and have freely chosen to stay in it when the question of a possible change arose. If I am a disturbing element, that is all right. I am not making a point of being that, but simply of saying what my conscience dictates and doing so without seeking my own interest. This means accepting such limitations as may be placed on me by authority, and not because I may or may not agree with the ostensible reasons why the limitations are imposed, but out of love for God who

> "In the name of lifeless and graven letters on parchment we are told that our life consists in the peaceful and pious meditation on Scripture and a quiet withdrawal from the world. But if one reads the prophets with his ears and eyes open he cannot help recognizing his obligation to shout very loud about God's will, God's truth, and justice of man to man."
> (Letter to Daniel Berrigan, November 27, 1962)

is using these things to attain ends which I myself cannot at the moment see or comprehend. I know He can and will in His own time take good care of the ones who impose limitations unjustly or unwisely. That is His affair and not mine. In this dimension I find no contradiction between love and obedience, and as a matter of fact it is the only sure way of transcending the limits and arbitrariness of ill-advised commands."[237]

Behind the silencing, he wrote a few weeks later, was the charge that he had been writing for "a communist-controlled publication," as *The Catholic Worker* was said to be by some of its opponents.[238]

In mid-May Merton received a letter from the Abbot General in which Dom Gabriel stressed the difference between religious orders which teach and those which pray. "I am not asking you to remain indifferent to the fate of the world," he insisted. "But I believe you have the power to influence the world by your prayers and by your life withdrawn into God more than by your writings. That is why I am not thinking about hurting the cause you are defending when I ask that you give up your intention of publishing the book you have finished, and abstain from now on from writing on the subject of atomic warfare, preparation for war, etc."[239]

Merton obeyed, if in a limited way. Never submitted to a publisher, the book remained generally unknown, but not entirely, for Merton again resorted to *samizdat* methods of communicating his views. With the Abbot's permission, several hundred copies of *Peace in the Post-Christian Era* were produced by mimeograph and mailed to friends who in turn shared their copies with others.[240] Though reaching far fewer readers than any of his other books, the text was studied all the more attentively by those who obtained it.[241] Merton was not altogether sorry about what had happened. He rejoiced in discovering access to uncensored channels of communication; he had become "a firm believer in the power of

Above:
(Photograph by Jim Forest, courtesy of Boston College, Burns Library)

*"It is unfortunate that so much of monastic obedience has become merely formal and trivial. There is no use in lamenting this, but nevertheless, renewal in this area must mean, above all, a recovery of the sense of obedience to God in all things and not just obedience to rules and superiors when obedience is demanded: and after that, go wool-gathering where you may!"*
(A Vow of Conversation)

the offbeat essay printed or mimeographed in a strange place."[242]

One of the problems with *Peace in the Post-Christian Era*, he realized, was that it had been written with a constant eye to what might be allowed through official channels. "What a mess one gets into," he wrote to me that July, "trying to write a book that will get through the censors, and at the same time say something. I was bending in all directions to qualify every statement and balance everything off, so I stayed right in the middle and perfectly objective ... [at the same time trying] to speak the truth as my conscience wanted it to be said."[243]

While relying on the mimeograph machine and publication in small journals, occasionally the uncensored Merton addressed wider audiences by writing for publication under pseudonyms. Under thin cover, one piece in *The Catholic Worker* was signed Benedict Monk. And to those acquainted with Merton's Marx Brothers sense of humor, who but Merton would sign himself Marco J. Frisbee?

Despite his problems with censorship, Merton was made hopeful by Pope John XXIII and the process of church renewal he had inspired. A Vatican Council, the first one in nearly a hundred years, had been announced by the Pope in January 1959 and began in October 1962. Though the first session was mainly devoted to revamping the liturgy, subsequent sessions were to consider such matters as the church's role in the modern world. In December 1962 Merton sent all his war-peace writing to Hildegard and Jean Goss-Mayr, secretaries of the International Fellowship of Reconciliation. The couple had received permission from Dom Gabriel Sortais to circulate Merton's peace essays among the theologians and bishops drafting a text on the church's social mission.

In April 1963, two months before his death, Pope John published what became the most widely dis-

*"The monk is the one supposedly attuned to the inner spiritual dimension of things. If he hears nothing and says nothing, then the renewal [of the Church] as a whole will be in danger and may be completely sterilized. But these authoritarian minds believe that the function of the monk is not to see or hear any new dimensions, simply to support the already existing viewpoints. ... The function of the monk ... then becomes simply to affirm his total support of officialdom."*
*(Letter to Jim Forest, April 29, 1962)*

Above:
The Second Vatican Council. (Photograph courtesy of Maryknoll archives)

cussed papal encyclical of modern times: *Pacem in Terris* (*Peace on Earth*). Stressing that the most basic human right is the right to life, John spoke out passionately against such threats to life as the arms race, said that war was no longer an apt means for vindicating violated rights, and called for legal protection of conscientious objectors to military service. Far from sanctioning blind obedience to those in authority, the Pope stressed the individual responsibility to protect life and uphold morality: "If civil authorities legislate or allow anything that is contrary to the will of God, neither the law made nor the authorization granted can be binding on the conscience of the citizens since God has more right to be obeyed than man." (nr. 51)

Days after the encyclical was released, Merton wrote the Abbot General to say "it was a good thing that Pope John didn't have to get his encyclical through our censors: and could I now start up again."[244] Specifically he asked Dom Gabriel for permission to return to work on *Peace in the Post-Christian Era* so that it might finally be published.

Unmoved, Dom Gabriel renewed the prohibition. Merton commented in his journal, "At the back of [Dom Gabriel's] mind obviously is an adamant conviction that France [of which Dom Gabriel was a citizen] should have the bomb and use it if necessary. He says that the encyclical [*Pacem in Terris*] has changed nothing in the right of a nation to arm itself with nuclear weapons for self-defense."[245]

In the summer of 1963 the silenced Merton was honored for what he had managed to publish before *Pacem in Terris* changed the direction of Catholic social thought. Awarded a medal by Pax, a Catholic peace group associated with the Catholic Worker, Merton wrote a letter of acceptance in which he commented that "a monastery is not a snail's shell nor is religious faith a kind of spiritual fallout shelter into which one can plunge to escape the criminal realities of an apocalyptic age." The monk, like anyone else, had to make decisions for or against life; these were, in fact, decisions for or against God. "I have attempted to say this in the past as opportunity has permitted, and opportunity has not permitted as much as I would have liked. But one thing I must admit: to say these things seems to me to be only the plain duty of any reasonable being. Such an attitude implies no heroism, no extraordinary insight, no special moral qualities, and no unusual intelligence. . . . These propositions are . . . clear as day light. . . . If I said it before *Pacem in Terris*, that still does not make me terribly original." The same was said, after all, "by Popes before Pope John, and by theologians, and by the Fathers of the Church, and by the Gospels themselves." Medals, he said, shouldn't be needed for those repeating ancient truths.[246]

In November 1963 Dom Gabriel Sortais died. The new Abbot General, Dom Ignatius Gillet, was, in time, to prove more open to Merton's peace writing.

# Pastor to Peacemakers

*Our job is to love others without stopping to inquire whether or not they are worthy. That is not our business. What we are asked to do is to love and this love will render both ourselves and our neighbors worthy, if anything can.*

Despite his membership in pacifist groups, Merton never rebuked those who resorted to violence in self-defense. He accepted the possibility that just war might have occurred in earlier times, when the technology of warfare didn't inevitably cause numerous noncombatant casualties, and might occur even in the modern context in the case of oppressed people fighting for liberation. But, as he wrote to Dorothy Day in 1962, the issue of the just war "is pure theory. . . . In practice all the wars that are [happening] . . . are shot through and through with evil, falsity, injustice, and sin so much so that one can only with difficulty extricate the truths that may be found here and there in the 'causes' for which the fighting is going on."[247]

Neither did he insist that a Christian was obliged to be a conscientious objector. Yet the highest form of Christian discipleship, he was convinced, required the renunciation of violence: "The Christian does not need to fight and indeed it is better that he should not fight, for insofar as he imitates his Lord and Master, he proclaims that the Messianic Kingdom has come and bears witness to the presence of the *Kyrios Pantocrator* [Lord of Creation] in mystery, even in the midst of the conflicts and turmoil of the

Opposite:
Merton during a retreat for peacemakers in 1965. (Photograph by Jim Forest, courtesy of Boston College, Burns Library)

*"Do not depend on the hope of results . . . These are not in your hands or mine, but they can suddenly happen, and we can share in them . . . The real hope . . . is not in something we think we can do, but in God who is making something good out of it in some way we cannot see. If we can do His will, we will be helping in this process. But we will not necessarily know all about it beforehand."*

*(Letter to Jim Forest, February 21, 1966)*

[149]

world."[248] What he found valuable in the just-war tradition was its insistence that evil must be actively opposed, and it was this that drew him to Gandhi, Dorothy Day, and groups involved in active nonviolent struggle for social justice like the Catholic Worker and the Fellowship of Reconciliation.

While his vocation made an active role in the peace movement impossible, through correspondence and occasional face-to-face visits Merton played a pastoral role among peace activists that was perhaps even more important than his public role as an author, and one in which he could communicate without having to worry about getting his words past the censors. Despite his isolation from events and his distance from centers of protest activity, he had a vivid memory of equivalent activities from his student days at Columbia. "I have the feeling of being a survivor of the shipwrecked thirties," he noted early in 1963, "one of the few that has kept my original face before this present world was born."[249]

What was often missing in the protest movements of the thirties and remained rare in similar movements of the sixties was compassion. Those involved in protest tend to become enraged with those they see as being responsible for injustice and violence and even toward those who uphold the status quo. But without compassion, Merton pointed out, the protester tends to become more and more centered in anger and may easily become an obstacle to changing the attitudes of others.

"We have to have a deep patient compassion for the fears of men, for the fears and irrational mania of those who hate or condemn us. . . . [These are, after all] the ordinary people, the ones who don't want war, the ones who get it in the neck, the ones who really want to build a decent new world in which there will not be war and starvation."[250]

Most people, Merton pointed out, are irritated or frightened by agitation even when it protests something — militarism, nuclear weapons, social injus-

*"We live in the time of no room, which is the time of the end . . . Into this world, this demented inn, in which there is absolutely no room for Him at all, Christ has come uninvited. But because He cannot be at home in it, because He is out of place in it, and yet He must be in it, His place is with those others for whom there is no room."*

(New Seeds of Contemplation)

[150]

tice—which objectively endangers them. "[People] do not feel at all threatened by the bomb ... but they feel terribly threatened by some ... student carrying a placard."[251]

Without love, especially love of opponents and enemies, he insisted that neither profound personal nor social transformation can occur.

Merton wrote to Dorothy Day in 1961:

Persons are not known by intellect alone, not by principles alone, but only by love. It is when we love the other, the enemy, that we obtain from God the key to an understanding of who he is, and who we are. It is only this realization that can open to us the real nature of our duty, and of right action. To *shut out* the person and to refuse to consider him as a person, as an other self, we resort to the impersonal "law" and to abstract "nature." That is to say we block off the reality of the other, we cut the intercommunication of our nature and his nature, and we consider only our own nature with its rights, its claims, its demands. And we justify the evil we do to our brother because he is no longer a brother, he is merely an adversary, an accused. To restore communication, to see our oneness of nature with him, and to respect his personal rights and his integrity, his worthiness of love, we have to see ourselves as similarly accused along with him ... and needing, with him, the ineffable gift of grace and mercy to be saved. Then, instead of pushing him down, trying to climb out by using his head as a stepping-stone for ourselves, we help ourselves to rise by helping him to rise. For when we extend our hand to the enemy who is sinking in the abyss, God reaches out to both of us, for it is He first of all who extends our hand to the enemy. It is He who "saves himself" in the enemy, who makes use of us to

Below:
Thomas Merton's sandals. (Photograph by Jim Forest, courtesy of Boston College, Burns Library)

*"The contemplative life has nothing to tell you except to reassure you and say that if you dare to penetrate your own silence and dare to advance without fear into the solitude of your own heart ... you will truly recover the light and capacity to understand what is beyond words and beyond explanations because it is too close to be explained ... "*
(The Monastic Journey)

recover the lost groat which is His image in our enemy.[252]

Where compassion and love are absent, actions that are superficially nonviolent tend to mask deep hostility, contempt, and the desire to defeat and humiliate an opponent. As he wrote in one of his most insightful letters:

> One of the problematic questions about nonviolence is the inevitable involvement of hidden aggressions and provocations. I think this is especially true when there are . . . elements that are not spiritually developed. It is an enormously subtle question, but we have to consider the fact that, in its provocative aspect, nonviolence may tend to harden opposition and confirm people in their righteous blindness. It may even in some cases separate men out and drive them in the other direction, away from us and away from peace. This of course may be (as it was with the prophets) part of God's plan. A clear separation of antagonists. . . . [But we must] always direct our action toward opening people's eyes to the truth, and if they are blinded, we must try to be sure we did nothing specifically to blind them.
>
> Yet there is that danger: the danger one observes subtly in tight groups like families and monastic communities, where the martyr for the right sometimes thrives on making his persecutors terribly and visibly wrong. He can drive them in desperation to be wrong, to seek refuge in the wrong, to seek refuge in violence. . . . In our acceptance of vulnerability . . . we play [on the guilt of the opponent]. There is no finer torment. This is one of the enormous problems of our time . . . all this guilt and nothing to do about it except finally to explode and blow it all out in hatreds, race hatreds,

Above:
Thomas Merton with Father Daniel Berrigan, S.J., a founder of the Catholic Peace Fellowship. (Photograph by Jim Forest, courtesy of Boston College, Burns Library)

*"Daniel Berrigan's visit was most stimulating. He is a man full of fire, the right kind, and a real Jesuit, of which there are not too many, perhaps . . . He is alive and full of spirit and truth. I think he will do much for the church in America and so will his brother Phil, the only priest so far to have gone on a Freedom Ride. They will have a hard time, though, and will have to pay for every step forward with their blood."*

(The Road to Joy)

political hatreds, war hatreds. We, the righteous, are dangerous people in such a situation. . . . We have got to be aware of the awful sharpness of truth when it is used as a weapon, and since it can be the deadliest weapon, we must take care that we don't kill more than falsehood with it. In fact, we must be careful how we "use" truth, for we are ideally the instruments of truth and not the other way around.[253]

Merton saw that the peace movement often tended to identify too much with particular political groups and ideologies. Ideally its actions should communicate liberating possibilities to others no matter how locked in they were to violent structures. He wrote late in 1962:

It seems to me that the basic problem is not political, it is apolitical and human. One of the most important things to do is to keep cutting deliberately through political lines and barriers and emphasizing the fact that these are largely fabrications and that there is another dimension, a genuine reality, totally opposed to the fictions of politics: the human dimension which politics pretends to arrogate entirely [to itself]. ... This is the necessary first step along the long way ... of purifying, humanizing and somehow illuminating politics.[254]

Peacemaking, he said, was rooted in spiritual life.

Above:
Fireplace in Merton's hermitage. (Photograph by Jim Forest)

We have to pray for a total and profound change in the mentality of the whole world. What we have known in the past as Christian penance is not a deep enough concept if it does not comprehend the special problems and dangers of the present age. Hair shirts will not do the trick, though there is no harm in mortifying the flesh. But vastly more important is the complete change of heart and the totally new outlook on the world of man. ... The great problem is this inner change. ... [Any peace action has] to be regarded ... as an application of spiritual force and not the use of merely political pressure. We all have the great duty to realize the deep need for purity of soul, that is to say the deep need to possess in us the Holy Spirit, to be possessed by Him. This takes precedence over everything else.[255]

He was convinced that engagement was made stronger by detachment. Not to be confused with disinterest in achieving results, detachment meant knowing that no good action is wasted even if the immediate consequences are altogether different from what one hoped to achieve.

In his longest letter on this theme, he advised:

Do not depend on the hope of results. When you are doing . . . an apostolic work, you may have to face the fact that your work will be apparently worthless and even achieve no result at all, if not perhaps results opposite to what you expect. As you get used to this idea, you start more and more to concentrate not on the results but on the value, the rightness, the truth of the work itself. And there too a great deal has to be gone through, as gradually you struggle less and less for an idea and more and more for specific people. The range tends to narrow down, but it gets much more real. In the end . . . it is the reality of personal relationships that saves everything. . . .

It is so easy to get engrossed with ideas and slogans and myths that in the end one is left holding the bag, empty, with no trace of meaning left in it. And then the temptation is to yell louder than ever in order to make the meaning be there again by magic. . . . As for the big results, these are not in your hands or mine, but they can suddenly happen, and we can share in them: but there is no point in building our lives on this personal satisfaction, which may be denied us and which after all is not that important. . . . The great thing, after all, is to live, not to pour out your life in the service of a myth: and we turn the best things into myths. If you can get free from the domination of causes and just serve Christ's truth, you will be able to do more and will be less crushed by the inevitable disappointments. . . . The real hope . . . is not in something we think we can do, but in God who is making something good out of it in some way we cannot see. If we can do His will, we will be helping in this process. But we will not necessarily know all about it beforehand.[256]

# Monk in the Rain

*Just get warm in any way you can and love God and pray.*

**A**s Merton struggled to define his responsibility for a world that seemed hurrying toward annihilation, the battle to come closer to his true self continued unabated.

His health was often a burden. Late in 1963 pain in his left arm and the base of his neck required traction at St. Joseph's Infirmary in Louisville. Treating other ailments, doctors prescribed an impressive array of pills. Merton was put on a special diet.

The world's health was even worse. America, burdened with racism and armed with the Cold War, seemed crowded with people primed to kill. The bombing of a black church in Birmingham in which four children perished deepened Merton's sense of identification with those who were the victims of violence; he put a photo of one of the children, 11-year-old Carol Denise McNair, in his journal. During hunting season the woods echoed with the cracks of rifle fire. There were flights of B-52 bombers flying high overhead each day with cargos of nuclear bombs and there was the rumble of cannon fire from Fort Knox many miles away. The fighting in Vietnam was beginning to boil into full-scale war. In November 1963 John F. Kennedy was shot dead in Dallas, while the following summer Harlem exploded in riots and three civil rights volunteers were murdered in Mississippi.

The turmoil of the sixties in both church and

Opposite:
(Photograph by John Lyons, courtesy of the Thomas Merton Studies Center)

*"What a thing it is to sit absolutely alone, in the forest, at night, cherished by this wonderful, unintelligible, perfectly innocent speech, the most comforting speech in the world, the talk that rain makes by itself all over the ridges, and the talk of the watercourses everywhere in the hollows! Nobody started it, nobody is going to stop it. It will talk as long as it wants, this rain. As long as it talks I am going to listen."*

(Raids on the Unspeakable)

[157]

world was pulling some experienced monks away from Gethsemani, among them Merton's confessor, Father John of the Cross. Like a child in the dark, Merton felt vulnerable, especially during periods on his own at the isolated hermitage where Dom James was allowing him more and more time. As the fall began he was sleeping there every night.

The publishing restrictions that the former Abbot General had imposed on Merton in 1962 were lifted by his successor in 1964. Some of the material Merton had circulated only in mimeographed form became the substance of a book issued that fall as *Seeds of Destruction*.

Merton read about Gandhi, in the process putting together a small book published in 1965 as *Gandhi on Nonviolence*. In an introductory essay Merton marveled at Gandhi's ability to see the oneness of the sacred and the secular and to join in his own life contemplative and active elements. Merton connected Gandhi with Pope John. Both men realized that "there can be no peace on earth without the

Left:
Firehoses turned on civil rights demonstrators in Birmingham, Alabama. (Photograph courtesy of Maryknoll archives)

*"The race question cannot be settled without a profound change of heart, a real shakeup and deep reaching metanoia on the part of White America. It is not just a question of a little more good will and generosity: it is a question of waking up to crying injustices and deep-seated problems which are ingrained in the present set-up and which instead of getting better are going to get worse."*

(Seeds of Destruction)

kind of inner change that brings man back to his 'right mind.' "[257]

A book by Hannah Arendt led Merton to consider the chief bureaucrat of the Holocaust, from which emerged his essay "A Devout Meditation in Memory of Adolf Eichmann." Eichmann, who had been declared sane by his examining psychiatrists, seemed to Merton an archetype of all those who were perfecters of efficient new technologies of killing—those for whom it was enough that those in authority required such methods. Merton wrote:

> The sanity of Eichmann is disturbing. We equate sanity with a sense of justice, with humaneness, with prudence, with the capacity to love and understand other people. We rely on the sane people of the world to preserve it from barbarism, madness, destruction. And now it begins to dawn on us that it is precisely the *sane* ones who are the most dangerous. It is the sane ones, the well-adapted ones, who can without qualms and without nausea aim the missiles and press the buttons that will initiate the great festival of destruction that they, the sane ones, have prepared. . . . No one suspects the sane, and the sane ones will have perfectly good reasons, logical, well-adjusted reasons, for firing the shot. They will be obeying sane orders that have come sanely down the chain of command.[258]

Merton the writer was being joined by Merton the artist. A "love affair" with photography began in the fall of 1964. Starting with a borrowed Kodak Instamatic, Merton used black-and-white film to photograph trees and tree stumps, paint buckets, the weathered side-board of old wooden buildings. Applying black ink to white paper, he used Japanese brushes to produce "calligraphs"—images, often abstract, that had in common with his photographs

Above:
Cover of *Gandhi on Nonviolence*, a volume edited by Merton and published by New Directions in 1965.

*"In Gandhi's mind, non-violence was not simply a political tactic which was supremely useful and efficacious in liberating his people from foreign rule . . . On the contrary, the spirit of non-violence sprang from an inner realization of spiritual unity in himself. The whole Gandhian concept of non-violent action and satyagraha is incomprehensible if it is thought to be a means of achieving unity rather than as the fruit of inner unity already achieved."*
(Gandhi on Non-Violence)

a remarkable and refreshing quiet. The images in both cases were "words out of silence." A first public exhibition of his calligraphs occurred in November, with another show soon after. Merton's purpose was to sell prints in order to found a scholarship for a black student. (With additional financial support provided by Dom James from monastery funds, the scholarship was created.)

Merton's exploration of the nonverbal may have been connected with his exploration of the feminine dimension of creation and of himself and his vocation. Certainly his sense of never having properly known women continued to haunt him, most of all in vivid dreams. In March 1964 he described a dream in which a distinguished woman Latinist from Harvard came to the monastery and "sang in Latin with meters, flexes and puncta." The novices giggled. Her presence, Merton realized when the Abbot entered the room, constituted a violation of the cloister. She had to be hustled out. Merton escorted her down the stairs noticing that, in her expulsion

Below:
(Photograph by Thomas Merton, courtesy of the Merton Legacy Trust)

*"There are drops of dew that show like sapphires in the grass as soon as the great sun appears, and leaves stir behind the hushed flight of an escaping dove."*

(The Sign of Jonas)

from the monastery, her clothes had become soiled and torn. "She was confused and sad"[259] — and so was Merton. Perhaps his Latin-speaking lady was a Western cousin of Proverb. Or perhaps she was the Latin liturgy, being swept away by the sixties' move to the vernacular in the Mass; Merton missed the Latin. In any event the dream suggests Merton's troubled awareness that there is something lop-sided about a males-only enclave. Eve was still the great temptress from whom men seeking salvation had to flee for their lives.

One night in late November he had dreamt of his beloved Proverb. She was a Chinese princess who had come to spend the day with him. Merton felt "overwhelmingly the freshness, the youth, the wonder, the truth of her, her complete reality, more real than any other, yet unobtainable."[260] The dream was also a recognition of the feminine wisdom of the Far East, which increasingly was opening itself to Merton.

Perhaps it was Proverb who made him so receptive to the Noah-like downpour that came the next night and which inspired one of Merton's finest essays, "Rain and the Rhinoceros." It was a celebration not only of rain but all that society ignores and neglects — at least until a price tag can be put on it. Merton recognized in rain a language of God. "Think of it: all that speech pouring down, selling nothing, judging nobody, drenching the thick mulch of dead leaves, soaking the trees, filling the gullies and crannies of the wood with water, washing out the places where men have stripped the hillside! . . . this wonderful, unintelligible, perfectly innocent speech, the most comforting speech in the world, the talk that rain makes."[261]

In the midst of rain and dreams Merton received a group of pacifists (I was one of them) for a retreat on "the spiritual roots of protest." Merton had arranged the event with the Fellowship of Reconciliation and its brand new off-shoot, the Catholic

Above:
(Photograph by John Lyons, courtesy of the Thomas Merton Studies Center)

*"Everything the Fathers of the Church say about the solitary life is exactly true. The temptations and the joys, above all, the tears and the ineffable peace and happiness. The happiness that is so pure because it is simply not one's own making but sheer mercy and gift. Happiness in the sense of having arrived at last in the place destined for me by God; of fulfilling the purpose for which I was brought here twenty-three years ago."*

(A Vow of Conversation)

Peace Fellowship, of which Merton was an advisor and sponsor. Merton's contribution to the four-day exchange focused on the "solitary witness" of Franz Jäggerstätter, an Austrian farmer who had been executed by the Nazis for refusing to serve in the army of the Third Reich. A devout Catholic, Jäggerstätter had received no support from his pastor or bishop; rather he was admonished that it was his duty to take the military oath. Who was he, a peasant, to take his conscience so seriously? For Merton, this married man and father was a saint uniquely matched to a century of total war. What bishops and theologians had refused to see was seen by a barely educated man who willingly gave up his life rather than collaborate in evil.[262]

On December 16 Merton had his first full day and night at the hermitage, coming down to the abbey only to say Mass and to eat a hot meal.

In the hermitage the night of January 30, 1965, the eve of his fiftieth birthday, Merton took fresh stock of himself. He was disturbed to recall the selfishness, glibness, and lack of love that had been typical of his relations with women throughout adolescence and adulthood. He had been "a damned fool" while at Clare College, Cambridge, "very self-ish and unkind to Joan." He recalled late nights with Sylvia on the steps of the Clare boat house. Was one of these women the mother of his child? He doesn't say, only remarking that profound shyness repeatedly had hidden "an urgent need for love."[263]

In the same journal entry he reaffirmed his vocation to solitude. His happiest moments in life had been while alone. Alone, he needed no masks. The joy given to him in those hidden places had allowed him to glimpse his real identity.

Yet he was not alone in his dreams. Early in February 1965 Merton dreamed about a black woman whom he recognized as his foster mother from a forgotten childhood. He owed her his life and love. "It was really she and not my natural mother who had given me life. ... Her face was ugly and severe, yet a great warmth came from her to me and we embraced with love. I felt deep gratitude, and what I recognized was not her face but the warmth of her embrace and of her heart. ... Then we danced a little together, I and my black mother."[264]

In June, wide awake, he remembered the Proverb-like Ann Winser, a 13-year-old girl he had seen briefly in his mid-teens while a guest of her older brother on the Isle of Wight. "I remember the quiet rectory in the shady valley of Brooke. She was the quietest thing in it. A dark and secret child. ... I hardly remember even thinking of her or noticing her, yet the other day I realized that I had never forgotten her and that she had made a deep impression." She represented "the part of the garden I never went to," the feeling that "if I had taken another turn in the road, I might have ended up married to Ann." She was the "true (quiet) woman with whom I never really came to terms in the world, and because of this, there remains an incompleteness in me that cannot be remedied."[265]

*"No matter what mistakes and delusions have marked my life, most of it I think has been happiness and, as far as I can tell, truth."*
(A Vow of Conversation)

# Father Louis, Hermit

*What more do I seek than this silence, this simplicity, this "living together with wisdom"?*

Hanging on the inside of the closet door in the hermitage was a Latin-inscribed sheet of parchment in which Pope Paul VI offered his blessing to "Father Louis, Hermit."

"The hermit project has been voted and approved officially by the Council of the community and is accepted and understood by most everyone," Merton wrote on August 20, 1965. "It begins officially tomorrow. I can use any prayers."[266] His only responsibilities within the community would be to say daily Mass in the library chapel, eat a hot meal at the infirmary, and give a lecture on Sundays that interested members of the community could attend.

"Life is this simple," he said in a final talk as Master of Novices. "We are living in a world that is absolutely transparent and God is shining through it all the time. This is not just a fable or a nice story. It is true. If we abandon ourselves to God and forget ourselves, we see it sometimes, and we see it maybe frequently. God manifests Himself everywhere, in everything—in people and in things and in nature and in events. It becomes very obvious that He is everywhere and in everything and we cannot be without Him. You cannot be without God. It's impossible. It's simply impossible. The only thing is that we don't see it. What is it that makes the world opaque? It is care."[267]

Leaving the novitiate and feeling blessedly free

Opposite:
Merton in the fall of 1965. (Photograph by Jim Forest, courtesy of Boston College, Burns Library)

*"I exist under trees, I walk in the woods out of necessity. I am both a prisoner and an escaped prisoner. I cannot tell you why, born in France, my journey ended here in Kentucky. It makes no difference. Do I have a 'day'? Do I spend my 'day' in a 'place'? I know there are trees here. I know there are birds here. I know the birds in fact very well, for there are precise pairs of birds (two each of fifteen or twenty species) living in the immediate area of my cabin. I share this particular place with them: we form an ecological balance."*

*("Day of a Stranger")*

from care, if only briefly, Merton picked up some old work clothes and walked up to his cinderblock hermitage, a rugged, austere building which lacked any plumbing. Water had to be carried. Merton shared the nearby wooden outhouse with a black snake.

"I am living as a stylite on top of a hermit hat," Merton wrote Bob Lax in October. "I am utterly alone from human company. . . . I make no more cookies in the cookie factory."[268]

Yet far from feeling settled down, Merton was never more willing to think about moving somewhere else than during those early months as a hermit at Gethsemani. As much as he had longed for radical solitude, its achievement was not without suffering. He often felt isolated and lonely. An invitation from Ernesto Cardenal asking for his participation in a monastic experiment at Solentiname in Nicaragua filled Merton with a longing to say yes. He wrote to Cardinal Paul Philippe, secretary of the Congregation of Religious in Rome, and to Pope Paul VI asking if he might be "loaned" to Solentiname while remaining a monk of Gethsemani. The response, while sympathetic, advised Merton to stay where he was. It was, of course, the answer he expected. He had been able to say yes to Cardenal and could blame his not actually going on Rome.

Merton's health took a turn for the worse. The most aggravating problem was dysentery, caused by pollution in a stream near the hermitage which had been Merton's initial source of water. He also suffered from dermatitis and for a time had to wear special dermal gloves.

While Merton was struggling with his new life as a hermit, on the other side of the world was the awful slaughter in Vietnam. One of those most sensitive to the war was Roger LaPorte, a former Cistercian novice who had become one of the young volunteers at the Catholic Worker in New York. Roger identified so deeply with those who were being burned alive by American bombs that on the

Above:
Pope Paul VI. (Photograph courtesy of Maryknoll archives)

*"In the refectory is read a message of the Pope, denouncing war, denouncing the bombing of civilians, reprisals on civilians, killing of hostages, torturing of prisoners (all in Vietnam). Do the people of this country realize who the Pope is talking about? They have by now become so solidly convinced that the Pope never denounces anybody but Communists that they have long since ceased to listen. The monks seem to know. The voice of the reader trembles."*

*("Day of a Stranger")*

[166]

night of November 9 he sat down in front of the United States Mission to the United Nations, poured gasoline on himself, struck a match, and became a voluntary victim of the war. He died of his burns two days later. It was an action none of his friends guessed Roger was planning.

When the news reached Gethsemani on November 11, Merton was stunned. He immediately telegrammed the Catholic Peace Fellowship office in New York:

> JUST HEARD ABOUT SUICIDE OF ROGER LAPORTE. WHILE I DO NOT HOLD CATHOLIC PEACE FELLOWSHIP RESPONSIBLE FOR THIS TRAGEDY, CURRENT DEVELOPMENTS IN PEACE MOVEMENT MAKE IT IMPOSSIBLE FOR ME TO CONTINUE AS SPONSOR OF FELLOWSHIP. PLEASE REMOVE MY NAME FROM LIST OF SPONSORS. THOMAS MERTON.

The Catholic Peace Fellowship, the peace group with which Merton was most engaged, was closely associated with the Catholic Worker.

"The spirit of this country at the present moment is to me terribly disturbing," he wrote me in a letter sent the same day. "It is not quite like Nazi Germany, certainly not like Soviet Russia, it is like nothing on earth I ever heard of before. This whole atmosphere is crazy, not just the peace movement, everybody. There is in it such an air of absurdity and moral void, even where conscience and morality are invoked (as they are by everyone). The joint is going into a slow frenzy. The country is nuts."[269]

A week later Merton reversed his decision, apologizing for his resignation. "I am, so to speak, making my novitiate as a 'hermit' of sorts and I have my hands full with this. It is a full time job just coping with one's own damn mind in solitude."[270]

Early in December Merton wrote:

> Roger's immolation started off a deep process of examination and it will lead far. Wrong as I

*"My own peculiar task in the church and in my world has been that of the solitary explorer who, instead of jumping on all the latest bandwagons at once, is bound to search the existential depths of truth in its silences, its ambiguities, and in those certainties which lie deeper than the bottom of anxiety . . . It is a kind of submarine life in which faith sometimes mysteriously takes on the aspect of doubt when, in fact, one has to doubt and reject conventional and superstitious surrogates that have taken the place of faith."*
(Faith and Violence)

think his act was objectively, I believe it did
not prejudice the purity of his own heart and I
never condemned him. What I condemned and
... still question is a pervasive ... spirit of irra-
tionality, of power seeking, of temptation to
the wrong kind of refusal and impatience and
to pseudo charismatic witness which can be
terribly, fatally destructive of all good. ...
[There is] a spirit of madness and fanaticism
[in the air] ... and it summons me to a deep
distrust of all my own acts and involvements in
this public realm. ... The real road [for me]
lies ... with a new development in thought
and work that will be, if it is what it should be,
much more true and more valid for peace than
any series of ephemeral gestures I might
attempt to make. But anyway, now is a time for
me of searching, digging and if I mention angst
it is not to dramatize myself in any way but to
assure you that I conceive my real and valid
union with you all to take this form of silently
getting ground up inside by the weights among
which you are moving outside. It is to be
understood that if I get any word, I hope reasonable word, to utter, I will not hesitate to
utter it as I have always done before.[271]

Through the Catholic Peace Fellowship he
released a press statement in December in which he
made public both the fact that he had become a
hermit and that he was remaining a sponsor of the
Catholic Peace Fellowship. He took the occasion to
express his conviction "that what we need most of
all today [in working for peace in Vietnam] is
patient, constructive and pastoral work rather than
acts of defiance which antagonize the average person
without enlightening him."

The crisis precipitated by Roger LaPorte's self-
immolation led Merton to write a major essay on
nonviolence, "Blessed Are the Meek." It was pub-

lished as a booklet by the Catholic Peace Fellowship in 1966.[272] Merton saw active nonviolence as a way of living the Sermon on the Mount. The meek whom Jesus identified as blessed are not the naturally quiet and obedient people who would never dare to protest. Rather, they are the ones who are meek before the word of God and who live in God's truth no matter what the cost. Nonviolence is a discipline, Merton stressed, of refusing to hate. It is a commitment to see the human face of an adversary, and to enter into dialogue. "The chief difference between nonviolence and violence," he commented, "is that the latter depends entirely on its own calculations. The former depends entirely on God and on his Word."[273]

In the midst of that stressful period a gift arrived which Merton regarded as a providential sign: an eighteenth-century hand-painted icon of the Virgin and Child. The donor, Marco Pallis, was a Buddhist friend in England with whom Merton had been corresponding since 1963. For Merton, the present was like a kiss from God. He wrote Pallis in response:

How shall I begin? I have never received such a precious and magnificent gift from anyone in my life. I have no words to express how deeply moved I was to come face to face with this sacred and beautiful presence granted to me. . . . At first I could hardly believe it. . . . It is a perfect act of timeless worship. I never tire of gazing at it. There is a spiritual presence and reality about it, a true spiritual "Thaboric" light, which seems unaccountably to proceed from the Heart of the Virgin and Child as if they had One heart, and which goes out to the whole universe. It is unutterably splendid. And silent. It imposes a silence on the whole hermitage. . . . [This] icon of the Holy Mother came as a messenger at a precise moment when a message was needed, and her presence before

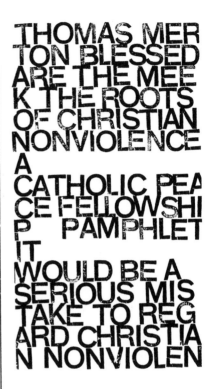

Above:
Cover of a pamphlet by Merton, "Blessed are the Peacemakers," issued by the Catholic Peace Fellowship.

*"Nonviolence must simply avoid the ambiguity of an unclear and confusing protest that hardens the warmakers in their self-righteous blindness. This means that in this case above all nonviolence must avoid a facile and fanatical self-righteousness, and refrain from being satisfied with dramatic, self-justifying gestures . . . Christian nonviolence . . . is convinced that the manner in which the conflict for truth is waged will itself manifest or obscure the truth."*

("Blessed are the Peacemakers")

me has been an incalculable aid in resolving a difficult problem.[274]

As 1966 began, though Merton still occasionally felt muddled and distracted, his hermitage life had achieved a certain rhythm and wholeness. He described an ordinary day in a letter to Abdul Aziz, a Sufi scholar with whom he had been corresponding since 1961. He got up about 2:30 in the morning to recite the normal psalm-centered offices of monastic prayer. Next came an hour or so of meditation followed by Bible reading. Then he made himself a light breakfast—tea or coffee, perhaps a piece of fruit or some honey. He read while eating, studying until about sunrise. With sunrise there was further prayer and then some manual work—sweeping, cleaning, cutting wood—until about 9 o'clock when he paused for another office of psalms. After that he wrote letters before going to the monastery to say Mass. Mass was followed by a cooked meal alone at

Below:
Thomas Merton's hermitage. (Photograph courtesy of the Abbey of Gethsemani)

*"I confess that I am sitting under a pine tree doing absolutely nothing. I have done nothing for one hour and firmly intend to continue to do nothing for an indefinite period. I have taken my shoes off. I confess that I have been listening to a mockingbird. Yes, I admit that it is a mockingbird. I hear him singing in those cedars, and I am very sorry. It is probably my fault. He is singing again. This kind of thing goes on all the time. Wherever I am, I find myself the center of reactionary plots like this one."*
("A Signed Confession of Crimes Against the State")

the monastery. Returning to the hermitage, he returned to reading, then said another office at 1 o'clock before another hour or more of meditation. Only then did he allow himself a period for writing, usually not more than an hour and a half. At about 4 o'clock he said another office of psalms and then made a light supper, typically tea or soup and a sandwich. After supper he had another hour of meditation before going to bed at around 7:30.

In the same letter Merton described his method of meditation:

Strictly speaking I have a very simple way of prayer. It is centered entirely on attention to the presence of God and to His will and His love. That is to say that it is centered on faith by which alone we can know the presence of God. One might say this gives my meditation the character described by the Prophet as "being before God as if you saw Him." Yet it does not mean imagining anything or conceiving a precise image of God, for to my mind this would be a kind of idolatry. On the contrary, it is a matter of adoring Him as invisible and infinitely beyond our comprehension, and realizing Him as all. . . . There is in my heart this great thirst to recognize totally the nothingness of all that is not God. My prayer is then a kind of praise rising up out of the center of Nothing and Silence. If I am still present "myself" this I recognize as an obstacle. . . . If He wills He can then make the Nothingness into a total clarity. If He does not will, then the Nothingness actually seems to itself to be an object and remains an obstacle. Such is my ordinary way of prayer or meditation. It is not "thinking about" anything, but a direct seeking of the Face of the Invisible. Which cannot be found unless we become lost in Him who is Invisible.[275]

"Your idea of me is fabricated with materials you have borrowed from other people and from yourself. What you think of me depends on what you think of yourself. Perhaps you create your idea of me out of material that you would like to eliminate from your own idea of yourself. Perhaps your idea of me is a reflection of what other people think of you. Or perhaps what you think of me is simply what you think I think of you."
(No Man is an Island)

# A Proverb Named Margie

*What is sweet about this bitter*
*Division? It is death*
*It is the devil's kingdom*
*We are two half people wandering*
*In two lost worlds.*[276]

**M**erton was suffering persistent back pain as 1966 began. On March 23 he entered St. Joseph's Hospital in Louisville for spinal surgery. Recovering from the operation a week later, he met a student nurse with gray eyes and long black hair who bore a striking resemblance to the original Proverb of his dreams. Her name was Margie.[277] They talked about *The Sign of Jonas,* the Peanuts comic strip, and *Mad* magazine. Merton quickly became dependent on her visits and their animated conversations. A few days later, when Margie left Louisville for a weekend in Chicago, Merton felt overwhelmed by loneliness. He lay awake half the night in his hospital bed tormented "by the gradual realization that we were in love and I did not know how I could live without her."[278] Before returning to the monastery he left a letter for her confiding his need for friendship and telling her how to write to him, marking the envelope "conscience matter" so that it wouldn't be read by anyone else at the abbey.

Thus began one of the most joyful and anguished periods of Merton's life.

Returning to the monastery April 10, he moved temporarily into the infirmary. He felt dazed. A week later there was a four-page letter from Margie.

Opposite:
Portrait of Merton by John Lyons. (Photograph courtesy of the Thomas Merton Studies Center)

*"When a wound is beginning to heal, they strip off the bandages, and the adhesive tape seems to take most of the skin with it . . . When a man becomes a Cistercian, he is stripped not only of his clothes, or part of his skin, but of his whole body and most of his spirit as well. And it is not all finished the first day: far from it! The whole Cistercian life is an evisceration, a gutting and scouring of the human soul."*
(Unpublished manuscript for
The Seven Storey Mountain,
from A Thomas Merton Reader)

Merton responded with a letter in which he said he had fallen in love with her. A few days later, ignoring monastery rules, he managed to reach her by telephone, making an appointment to see her on April 26, when he would be in Louisville for a post-operative examination. They had lunch in a local restaurant where Merton showed her a poem he had written for her, "The World in My Bloodstream." (Seventeen more poems for Margie were to follow.) Margie told Merton he didn't know what he was getting into, while Merton assured her that they could love each other without a sexual relationship. They could aim for spiritual love. The rest could be controlled, Merton assured her.

On May 5 James Laughlin and Chilean poet Nicanor Parra came to visit Merton. They had a picnic not far from the abbey. Using Laughlin's loose change, Merton called Margie from a pay phone along the road, arranging for Margie to join them for a meal later in the day. The four of them ate in the Luau Room at the Louisville airport. Merton, unshaven and wearing tee-shirt and overalls, must have been the oddest sight in the restaurant in many a day — looking like a convict, he noted in his journal, and probably feeling like one too. With Merton concentrating his attention mainly on her, it must have been awkward for Margie. Finally Merton and Margie went off for a walk, then sat for a while on a knoll of grass at the edge of the airport, in view of others but to some extent alone. "Suppose the clear light of that evening were love itself," Merton wrote of their time together that day, "and suppose we just became that light, that love: as if the clear beauty of the evening incarnated itself and its beauty and its meaning in us . . . and the meaning of everything that ever happened was suddenly centered in us because we were now love. It was our turn to express and show forth in worship the essence of all truth and life and meaning by our love."

"Thomas Merton had found his authentic whole-

*"All monks, as is well known, are unmarried, and hermits more unmarried than the rest of them. Not that I have anything against women. I see no reason why a man can't love God and a woman at the same time. If God was going to regard women with a jealous eye, why did he go and make them in the first place?"*

*("Day of a Stranger")*

ness in authentic love," comments Michael Mott.[279] Margie was for Merton the one person with whom he could be himself without a facade. For the first time in his remembered life, Merton felt he was wholly known not only by God but by another person. "This is God's own love He makes in us," he wrote in a poem that night.[280] In his journal he wondered about the possibility of "chaste marriage."

Together again on May 7 for a picnic with several friends on the edge of Dom Frederic's Lake on the monastery grounds, they managed to have a walk together. Merton tried to explain that he was a person who needed to live alone, while at the same

Below:
Thomas Merton seated at the edge of Monk's Pond on the monastery grounds. (Photograph courtesy of the Thomas Merton Studies Center)

time feeling he couldn't live apart from her. As they sat on the embankment of a creek, they imagined Merton getting a job in Louisville, buying a car, and being together whenever they wanted. That night Merton wrote of his awareness that he too "could love with an awful completeness." His definition of the meaning of the vow of chastity was shrinking steadily. Yet he was aware that, while he was drifting further and further from what was expected of him as a monk living under vows, he was intensely alive, not least when praying. In a poem he asked, "Why has God created you to be in the center of my being?"[281]

In Louisville May 14 for medical reasons, he had lunch with Margie. Besides sharing their enthusiasm for Joan Baez's ballad "Silver Dagger," they talked about what living together might mean. ("Silver Dagger" became a binding song for them. Merton had a record player in the hermitage. They each played the song at 1:30 A.M., when Margie's shift at the hospital was finished. Merton's time of rising was brought forward an hour.)

Five days later they met for a walk and picnic in the woods near Vineyard Knob, on the grounds of Gethsemani but well off the community's beaten track, sharing a bottle of wine that Margie had brought for the occasion.

Joy and guilt followed each other in quick succession just as fantasies of marriage alternated with decisions to bring their relationship to an end so that he could get on with his vocation as it was supposed to be lived.

Frightened by where the momentum of love was taking them, Merton called off plans for another meeting a few days later. He had now returned to his hermitage from the infirmary and was face-to-face with the terrible choice that had to be made.

Their next meeting was in the safe confines of Cunningham's restaurant in Louisville in connection with another doctor's visit by Merton. Both sensed

*"Love is our true destiny. We do not find the meaning of life by ourselves alone — we find it with another. We do not discover the secret of our lives merely by study and calculation in our own isolated meditations. The meaning of our life is a secret that has to be revealed to us in love, by the one we love."*

(Love and Living)

the climate of their relationship had changed. "I can never be anything else but a solitary," Merton wrote in his journal that night. "My loneliness is my ordinary climate. That I was allowed to have so many moments of complete accord and harmony and love with another person, with her, was simply extraordinary. I like people, but usually I am tired of being with others after about an hour. That I could be with her for hours and hours and not be tired for an instant with her—it was a miracle, but it did not mean that I was not essentially a solitary."

A week later they met again in Louisville, this time at the office of Merton's friend, psychiatrist Jim Wygal, despite his disapproval of what Merton was doing. For Merton's part, he was freshly aware of how deeply he loved Margie and how empty the future seemed when he imagined it without her.

Aware that his vow of chastity was going up in smoke, he went to his confessor, for the first time revealing to a brother monk the great event going on in his life. Despite this, as became clear when Merton managed to call Margie later that day, the idea of marriage kept charging back across all his arguments and resolutions.

Part of another call to Margie the next day, June 12, happened to be overheard by the monk running the switchboard; he felt it his duty to inform Dom James, as Merton learned from the cellarer the next day. As no one knew better than Merton, something like this was bound to happen in a tiny monastic village. There was as much relief as anxiety in his response to the news.

Not waiting for the Abbot to summon him, Merton went to see Dom James and told him in general terms what was going on, refusing however to reveal Margie's name. Merton was astonished and relieved with Dom James's reaction. He didn't hit the ceiling but responded with warmth and concern, only urging Merton to make a complete break. It wasn't an entirely candid conversation on Merton's side—he

denied that he was thinking about marriage, though this had been exactly what Margie and Merton had been talking about on the phone. Dom James wondered if it would help Merton to return for a time to the community, perhaps living in the infirmary, but gave his blessing to Merton remaining in the hermitage.

Merton called Margie to tell her what had happened—something they both had expected sooner or later. She was appalled by how inhuman it all was. Merton wrote a bitter poem about being careful with love for "it fills the world with destruction / Millions of small pocket cyclones / Have fouled up communication with / Inexhaustible demanding rage. . . ."[282]

The next day Dom James told Merton that it wasn't just advice not to have any more contact with "that woman." It was an order.

On June 22 Merton resolved that the "whole thing has to be given up."

Dreaming two nights later, he saw his mother's face appearing in a tangle of dark briars behind luminous roses with silky petals, an image contrasting with his briars-only portrait of her in *The Seven Storey Mountain*. Margie had shifted his way of seeing women, even his own mother. Then he dreamed that, while in the hospital, he was "short and rude" with a student nurse: an "ideal" celibate defending his vow of chastity but hardly the sort of human being Merton longed to be.

Despite the Abbot's order, it seemed to Merton a requirement of charity to see Margie face-to-face one more time. In Louisville for X-rays on June 25, Merton met her and found her distraught. She had decided to seek a job in the hospital of her hometown where she planned to volunteer her services in "special cases"—work involving sacrifice. Merton gave her *A Midsummer Diary*, written during the past ten days. It had the caustic subtitle, "Or the account of how I once again became untouchable."

While he wondered if he would ever see her again when they parted that day, they were together again July 16 when Merton was in Louisville for treatment of a sprained ankle. She picked him up at the doctor's office and they went off with a bag of cherries for a picnic in Cherokee Park. It was one of their happiest visits despite the awful awareness that a future together was hopeless. "We rock and swim / In love's wordless pain," Merton wrote in a poem about the day. "Halfway between / Heaven and hell / Zion and the green river / We rock together / In that lovely desperate grip . . ."[283]

Dom James talked with Merton again July 28, not about Margie but about other indications of disarray in Merton's life: an unauthorized visit to the nearby convent of the Sisters of Loretto, and a swim Merton had taken with a visitor in one of the monastery ponds. Wondering if the strain of the hermitage wasn't too much, Dom James again suggested returning to life in community. Perhaps Merton could

"When people are truly in love, they experience far more than just a mutual need for each other's company and consolation. In their relation with each other they become different people: they are more than their everyday selves, more alive, more understanding, more enduring, and seemingly more endowed. They are made more into new beings. They are transformed by the power of their love."

(Love and Living)

teach scripture as Master of Juniors? The main effect of the meeting was to make real to Merton the fact that his vocation as hermit was at risk.

Meeting again a week later, Dom James teased Merton about his relationship with Margie, which Dom James imagined was entirely over. The Abbot said he should write a book called *How to Get Hermits into Heaven*. Merton was furious. On leaving Dom James's office, Merton said, "When the baby is born you can be the godfather!" Dom James took it as a joke, but Merton saw the worry on his face.

Rather than risk seeing Margie again, Merton sent her a letter "saying in effect Goodbye." She was due to graduate and would soon be leaving Louisville. Imagining her opening the letter and reading it, he was stricken, tried in vain to reach her by phone, then wrote her a poem. He felt howls of pain "rending their way up out of the very ground of my being. . . . I thought I was being torn in half." A week later, when he managed to reach her by phone, he learned that letters she had sent him were not getting through even though marked "conscience matter." Her voice, he wrote in his journal, was choked with emotion.

On September 8, following a private retreat, Merton made a permanent commitment to a hermit's vocation: "I, Brother M. Louis Merton, solemnly professed monk of the Abbey of Our Lady of Gethsemani, having completed a year of trial in the solitary life, hereby make my commitment to spend the rest of my life in solitude in so far as my health may permit." Dom James signed as a witness.

Even then Merton and Margie managed two brief, final visits in late October. Margie was in Louisville for exams and Merton was staying at St. Anthony's Hospital for treatment of intestinal troubles. After that there was only very occasional contact by telephone; Merton's last call to Margie was a few months before his death.

In the end, Merton renewed his commitment to

*Don't sing love songs*
*You'll wake my mother*
*She's sleeping here*
*Right by my side,*
*And in her right hand*
*A silver dagger*
*She says that I can't*
*be your bride.*

*Go court another tender maiden*
*And hope that she will be your wife*
*For I've been warned and I've decided*
*To sleep alone all of my life.*
("Silver Dagger," traditional
Appalachian ballad)

remain a monk and to persevere as a hermit, the most difficult choice of his life. His love for Margie hadn't ended. In his soul, and probably in hers, there had been a kind of wedding. A man with no sense of the impossible, Merton had crashed full-speed, but even so a kind of healing had happened to him. "There is something deep, deep down inside us, darling, that tells us to let go completely," he had written in a letter to Margie that summer, though it is unclear whether the letter was ever sent. "Not just the letting go when the dress drops to the floor and bodies press together with nothing between, but the far more thrilling surrender when our very being surrenders itself to the nakedness of love and to a union where there is no veil of illusion between us."

What had occurred that summer was known only to a few friends, most of them quite worried by what was going on. Yet it wasn't Merton's intention that it remain a secret. Copies of the poems were given to James Laughlin for safekeeping and eventual publication. The journals became part of the archive of the Merton Literary Trust that Merton had set up with Father John Loftus at Bellarmine College in Louisville. Though publication of some material was to be delayed for twenty-five years after his death, he wanted nothing suppressed, including his love for Margie: "It needs to be known too, for it is part of me. My need for love, my loneliness, my inner division, the struggle in which solitude is at once a problem and a 'solution.' And perhaps not a perfect solution either."

*We are beyond the ways of the far ships*
*Here in this coral port,*
*Farther than the ways of fliers,*
*Because our destinies have suddenly transported*
*    us*
*Beyond the brim of the enamel world.*
*        (Figures for an Apocalypse)*

[181]

# A Member of the Family

*The responsibility of presiding over anything larger than a small chicken coop is beyond my mental, moral and physical capacities.*

As 1967 began, Merton sent out a mimeographed letter to friends in which he commented that he was becoming more conscious of "the futility of a life wasted in argument when it should be given entirely to love." He hoped he would "be able to give up controversy some day."[284]

A new kind of love began making its way into his life. A spark of friendship with Frank and Tommie O'Callaghan blazed so warmly that Merton became, in effect, not only a frequent guest in their large, child-crowded home but a member of the family. Often in Louisville for medical appointments, Merton's main place of refuge was the O'Callaghan house, eating there, playing with the children, sometimes staying the night. In warm weather he occasionally joined in family picnics. A similar bond was formed in Bardstown with Thompson and Virginia Willett, another couple with lots of children. If Merton was not to marry, at least he was able to experience a steady familial warmth.

An aspect of Merton's attraction to both families was the vital Catholicism he found in these households, neither rigidly conservative nor rabidly modern and "progressive." Merton felt especially out of gear with the new breed of progressive Catholics, one of whose tenets was that the only place for a monk in the modern world was a prison cell. One

Left:
Merton on a "family picnic" with Sister Therese Lentfoehr and Tommie O'Callaghan. (Photographs courtesy of Tommie O'Callaghan)

*"Another of your most important duties [as a designated trustee of Merton's literary estate] will be to see that the author, during his declining years, is occasionally revived by picnics. And that he has access to suitable sources of creative inspiration from time to time."*
(Letter to Tommie O'Callaghan, October 17, 1967)

[183]

radical author wrote to say that the monastic life was unchristian, subhuman, and demonic. "Mark my words," Merton warned Bob Lax concerning the progressive Catholic, "there is no uglier species on the face of the earth . . . mean, frivolous, ungainly, inarticulate, venomous, and bursting at the seams with progress into the secular cities and the Teilhardian subways. The Ottavianis [a cardinal whose name was synonymous with conservatism] are bad but these are infinitely worse."[285]

He found many changes in the liturgy at best funny, at worst tasteless and ugly. He could hardly believe his ears when the monks started to sing "The Church's One Foundation" at a service of profession for a new member of the community: "Renewal? For me it's a return to the deadly past. Victorian England."

[184]

Bursitis forced another operation on Merton in late February. Because he was troubled with allergies, Merton's doctor banned beer, beef, and dairy products. To make hermitage life physically less demanding for Merton, Dom James arranged for plumbing to be installed. By the summer Merton had a sink, running water, water heater, hot plate, and refrigerator.

As the months passed there was a steady trickle of visitors, among them Islamic scholar Sidi Abdeslam, philosopher Jacques Maritain, singer and peace activist Joan Baez, various writers and theologians — Jonathan Williams, Guy Davenport, Will Campbell, James Holloway, Rosemary Haughton, and Walker Percy — and such friends as Bob Lax, Sy Freedgood, Naomi Burton Stone, Dan Berrigan, John Howard Griffin, Ralph Eugene Meatyard, and Ron Seitz.

One gets a glimpse of Merton shortly after his fifty-second birthday in an essay in which Guy Davenport describes the best display of manners on the part of restaurant staff he had ever witnessed. The venue was the Imperial Ramada Inn in Lexington, Kentucky. Gathered around the table were "the photographer Ralph Eugene Meatyard (disguised as a businessman), the Trappist Thomas Merton (in mufti, dressed as a tobacco farmer with a tonsure), and an editor of *Fortune* [none other than Merton's old friend, Sy Freedgood] who had wrecked his Hertz car coming from the airport and was covered with spattered blood from head to toe. Hollywood is used to such things (Linda Darnell having a milk shake with Frankenstein's monster between takes), and Rome and New York, but not Lexington, Kentucky. Our meal was served with no comment whatever by the waitresses, despite Merton downing six martinis and the *Fortune* editor stanching his wounds with all the napkins."[286]

While company was always stimulating, Merton's travel itch remained intense. Dom James, however, was more reluctant than ever to bless anything more

*"Go on then and educate me in pop music. I don't know much about pop music. I am a confirmed jazzman, but I need to know more about pop also. Like some of those outfits you have out there that I hear such a lot about — Grateful Dead and all that — tell me about them and send me your number on the Monterey thing . . . What kind of pop music do I like? I haven't heard much but on one of the latest Dylan records I like 'Obviously Five Believers,' for instance (that's on the album 'blonde on bl.'). That strikes me as inspired, shamanic, and everything. On the Beatles record I like 'Taxman' and all the rest too."*

*(Letter to Suzanne Butorovitch, a sixteen-year-old high school student who invited Merton to contribute to her school's "underground" newspaper)*

than brief local outings. When Merton told Dom James in January 1967 about an invitation to visit the Trappist abbey of Melleray in France, the Abbot responded, "God has given you this hermitage not to quit it for greater expansion of exterior activities, but to remain in it for a greater deepening of your interior activities."[287]

Despite his aches, pains, and occasional disappointments, Merton was in good spirits. His sense of humor was evident not only in letters but even in photos. With a borrowed Nikon, he took a photo in April showing a heavy construction skyhook hanging over the Kentucky countryside. "The only known photograph of God," Merton noted on the back.

While only allowing himself a couple of hours a day for writing and editing, in those small spaces he achieved a great deal, including a series of literary studies focusing on Albert Camus, William Faulkner, William Styron, and Simone Weil.[288] There was also his essay on Ishi, the last surviving member of a tribe of native Americans in California.[289] He produced new essays on monastic life and the contemplative vocation[290] as well as a preface for the Japanese edition of *The New Man*.[291] He edited *A Vow of Conversation*, his journal of 1964-65, but decided to hold off publication, partly because he was sure the book would provoke a rash of critical reviews—not so much of the book as of himself—from progressive Catholics who would consider a hermit's vocation irrelevant if not counter-revolutionary. Soon after that he finished *Zen and the Birds of Appetite*. A frequent contributor to small magazines, that year he launched one of his own, *Monks Pond*, the first of four issues appearing in December 1967.[292]

There were also his Sunday lectures at the monastery, mainly drawn from notes on his current reading. The Sufi movement within Islam and the Cargo Cults of the South Pacific were among the major topics.[293]

Below:
Cover of *Zen and the Birds of Appetite*, published by New Directions in 1968.

*Ride your horse along the edge of the sword.*
*Hide yourself in the middle of the flames.*
*Blossoms of the fruit tree will bloom in the fire.*
*The sun rises in the evening.*

(Zen Saying)

Zen and the Birds of Appetite
Thomas Merton

During restricted daily periods for correspondence, letters issued from his typewriter like snowflakes in a blizzard. Suzanne Butorovich, only 16 when she sent her first letter in June 1967, became one of his favorite correspondents. She asked Merton if he liked pop music and what he thought of the Beatles and LSD. (Merton liked the Beatles song "Taxman," recommended Bob Dylan's latest album, and said he didn't need LSD because "the birds turn me on." A later letter to her revealed his method of cooking kasha.[294])

In letters to June Yungblut, a Quaker living in Atlanta, he prepared for a retreat at Gethsemani for civil rights activists that was to involve Martin Luther King, but the event perished with Dr. King's assassination.

One of the great joys of 1967 was the ordination of Dan Walsh, the person who first told Merton about the Abbey of Gethsemani and made him consider a vocation with the Trappists. Walsh had been a longtime resident in the monastery guest house. It had been the idea of the Archbishop of Louisville that this dedicated theologian ought to become a priest. The event occurred at St. Thomas Seminary May 16, followed by a big party at the O'Callaghan house. Merton was among the most festive. "There was a lot of celebrating," Merton wrote in a letter. "In fact I celebrated on too much champagne, which is a thing a Trappist rarely gets to do, but I did a very thorough job. At one point in the afternoon I remember looking up and focusing rather uncertainly upon four faces of nuns sitting in a row looking at me in a state of complete scandal and shock. Another pillar of the Church had fallen."[295]

Still more important was the permission Merton received from Dom James to celebrate Mass in the hermitage. Using a specially made cedarwood altar, Merton said his first Mass there on July 16, the Feast of Our Lady of Carmel, to whom the hermitage was dedicated. The hermitage now sheltered

Above:
Merton called this "the only known photograph of God." (Photograph by Thomas Merton, courtesy of the Merton Legacy Trust)

every aspect of Merton's life. (Early in 1968 a six-by-eight-foot chapel was added to the hermitage.)

In September 1967 Dom James made the startling announcement that he was retiring. He had decided to follow Merton's example and become a hermit, the monastery's third. (The second was Father Flavian Burns.) Alarmed at the thought that he might be elected as Dom James's successor, Merton posted a statement on the community bulletin board—"My campaign Platform for non-Abbot and permanent keeper of my present doghouse"—in which he assured everyone that "the responsibility of presiding over anything larger than a small chicken coop is beyond my mental, moral and physical capabilities." He made known that he had once taken a private

Below:
Merton, assisted by Brother Maurice Flood, gives communion to Jacques Maritain. Kneeling at the left is Merton's old professor, Daniel Walsh. (Photograph by John Howard Griffin, courtesy of the Thomas Merton Studies Center)

vow against ever accepting abbatial office. In any event he wasn't equipped, he declared, to cope with 125 confused and anxiety-ridden monks. Further, his ideas on monastic development had become foggy due to the encroachments of age and mental deterioration. If elected, however, he promised plenty of beer.[296]

If not an abbot, Merton proved to be something of an abbot-maker, helping convince his fellow hermit, Father Flavian Burns, to stand. Merton worried that Dom James's successor might be ill-disposed to hermits and therefore wanted a candidate who was sure to let the hermits continue. When the monks cast their votes on January 13, 1968, Father Flavian was chosen by a large majority. But a week before the event Merton had made a firm decision that he would remain a monk of Gethsemani no matter who was chosen, holding on just as Pasternak had clung to Russia, refusing to leave no matter how severe the political (or theological) weather might be. He had not come to Gethsemani, he recalled, to have his own way.

Dom Flavian had an entirely different understanding of his office than Dom James and a readiness to let Merton accept some of the invitations he received.

"The paradox is that it is to a great extent because I am here that I am invited to go," he had told one correspondent, "while it is because I am here I can't go."[297] Under Dom Flavian a new era dawned in Merton's life. He had the chance to become a travelling hermit. Merton was in the long-awaited, exhilarating but also quite alarming position of having no one to say no on his behalf.

"People ask me if now that we have a new Abbot, I will be able to 'get out' more. Will I be able to visit campuses and engage in conferences and dialogue, etc.? . . . For my part, I do not think that even if it were possible for me, I would be justified in going around appearing in public, or semi-public, and giving talks. I feel it would not be consistent with my real vocation . . . I am committed to a life of solitude and meditation which I hope I can share with others by a certain amount of writing. And that is about it."

(Circular Letter to Friends, Pre-Lent 1968)

# Asia on My Mind

*I have my own way to walk and for some reason or other Zen is right in the middle of it wherever I go.*

**M**ost invitations were easily turned down, but one that came at the beginning of 1968 seemed heaven-sent: Would Merton come to Asia in December to take part in a conference of Benedictine and Trappist abbots near Bangkok? Late in March Merton told Dom Flavian that he would like to accept and, while travelling, visit "some Zen places" elsewhere in Asia. Though with hesitation, Dom Flavian eventually agreed.[298]

Merton had been attentive to Asia since he was 15, when he had taken Gandhi's side in student debate. Living in New York seven years later, a Hindu monk from India, Bramachari, had deeply impressed Merton, as had A. K. Coomaraswamy's writings on art and asceticism. While drafting his dissertation on William Blake, Merton had discovered Chuang Tzu, the Chinese storytelling sage who had lived several hundred years before Christ.

In the late fifties Merton's thinking led him back toward Asia. In 1956 he had begun reading everything he could find by D. T. Suzuki, the Japanese Zen Buddhist scholar. Three years later Merton initiated a correspondence with Suzuki, confessing he did not pretend to understand Zen but nonetheless owed a great debt to Suzuki. "Time after time, as I read your pages, something in me says, 'That's it!' Don't ask me what. I have no desire to explain it to

Opposite:
Thomas Merton with Thich Nhat Hanh, a Vietnamese Buddhist monk. (Photograph by John Heidbrink)

*"He is more my brother than many who are nearer to me in race and nationality, because he and I see things in exactly the same way . . . Do what you can for him. If I mean something to you, then let me put it this way; do for Nhat Hanh whatever you would do for me if I were in his position. In many ways I wish I were."*
(Faith and Violence)

anybody. . . . So there it is, in all its beautiful purposelessness."[299] He wondered whether, should Suzuki come to the United States, he might not visit the Abbey of Gethsemani? Merton had permission to meet Suzuki in that event. He took the occasion to send Suzuki a collection of sayings of the Desert Fathers, the Zen Masters of the early church.

While Suzuki never came to Gethsemani, in 1964 Dom James had allowed Merton a short trip to New York to meet Suzuki, then age 94 and deaf but still the lively, responsive man Merton had anticipated. They drank green tea and talked. The main thing for Merton was "to see and experience the fact that there really is a deep understanding between myself and this extraordinary and simple man whose books I have been reading now for about ten years with great attention." Suzuki told Merton a story about a great master's dream in which his mother appeared to him with two mirrors, one in each sleeve. One was black, the other contained all things; the master found "himself among them, looking out." Being with Suzuki and his assistant, Miss Okamura, Merton "felt as if I had spent a few moments with my own family." They reminded him of his friends in Kentucky, Victor and Carolyn Hammer, among people especially linked in Merton's life with *Hagia Sophia*.[300]

Suzuki's essays had revived Merton's interest in Chuang Tzu. In 1961 he had enlisted the help of John Wu in preparing *The Way of Chuang Tzu*. "I have enjoyed writing this more than any other I can remember. . . . I simply like Chuang Tzu because of what he is," Merton commented in the book's preface.

In the midst of the period in which Merton was grappling with his longing to marry Margie, he had a visit from Thich Nhat Hanh, a Buddhist monk, Zen Master, and poet from Vietnam. Accompanied by John Heidbrink of the Fellowship of Reconciliation staff, Nhat Hanh spent two days at Gethsemani at the end of May 1967. Merton immediately recognized Nhat Hanh as someone very like himself. For

Below:
Cover of *The Way of Chuang Tzu*, published in 1965 by New Directions.

*When Chuang Tzu was about to die, his disciples began planning a splendid funeral.*
*But he said: "I shall have heaven and earth for my coffin; the sun and moon will be the jade symbols hanging by my side; . . . What more is needed?"*
*But they said: "We fear that crows and kites will eat our Master."*
*"Well," said Chuang Tzu, "above ground I shall be eaten by crows and kites, below it by ants and worms. In either case I shall be eaten. Why are you so partial to birds?"*
(The Way of Chuang Tzu)

# THE WAY OF CHUANG TZU

### THOMAS MERTON

Merton it was like meeting Chuang Tzu in the flesh. As the two monks talked, the different religious systems in which they were formed didn't seem to matter. "Thich Nhat Hanh is my brother," Merton said in writing a preface for a book on the Vietnam War by Nhat Hanh. "He is more my brother than many who are nearer to me in race and nationality, because he and I see things exactly the same way." When Merton asked Nhat Hanh what the war was doing to Vietnam, the Buddhist said simply, "Everything is destroyed." This, Merton said to the monks at his Sunday lecture, was truly a monk's answer, revealing the essence without wasting a word. Merton described the rigorous formation of Buddhist monks in Vietnam and the fact that instruction in meditation doesn't begin early. "Before you can learn to meditate," he said, quoting Nhat Hanh, "you have to learn how to close the door." The monks laughed; they were used to the reverberation of slamming doors as latecomers hurried to church.

In 1967 Dan Berrigan had suggested Merton go to Vietnam as a "hostage for peace," using his presence as a human shield, making the place where he was living less likely to be bombed. Merton had been haunted with the idea and was willing in principle to take part though the project never materialized.

For fifteen years Asian religion had figured largely in his reading, writing and talks within the community. Now he had the chance to *be* in Asia. He even wondered if Asia might not be the place to live — perhaps a hermitage in the Himalayas? Dom Flavian expressed openness to members of the community, while remaining part of Gethsemani, to live in remote places, though within the USA.

Gethsemani no longer seemed to Merton far enough off the beaten path; sometimes he felt he was living next to a highway intersection. In April, just two days after the murder of Martin Luther King, Jr., a visitor describing herself as the Woman in Revelation (a "problematic apocalyptic woman," Merton

*"What is the driving power behind the massive stupidity in Vietnam, with its huge expense and its absurd effects? It is the obsession of the American mind with the myth of know-how, and with the capacity to be omnipotent. Once this is questioned, we will go to any lengths, ANY lengths to resolve the doubt that has thus been raised in our minds . . . We are learning how bestial and how incredible are the real components of that myth. Vietnam is the psychoanalysis of the U.S."*

(The Hidden Ground of Love)

[193]

noted in his journal) found her way to his hermitage. There had been other unexpected and unknown people turning up. Merton had good reason to wonder, in an America in which so many people were armed, whether the day might come when he was confronted by a visitor with a gun. An intercom was installed linking the hermitage to the monastery.

He was also troubled about the problem of staying in the United States and thus, as he wrote to his Belgian Benedictine friend, Jean Leclercq, "to some extent remaining identified with a society which I believe to be under the judgment of God and in some sense under a curse for the crimes of the Vietnam War." He wondered aloud again about the possibility of becoming part of a small monastic community in Nicaragua or Chile. Yet he didn't see how leaving his adopted country would be fully honest either for "if this society is under judgment, I too should remain and sustain myself the judgment of everyone else, since I am after all not that much different from the others. The question of sin is a great one today—I mean collective guilt for crimes against humanity."[301]

On May 6 Merton flew to the West Coast to visit the Trappist monastery of Our Lady of Redwoods in Eureka, California. Besides giving several talks to the nuns, he explored the immediate area to see if there was a suitable place there for one or several hermitages. The most inviting spot was Bear Harbor, though Merton was alarmed by the number of cars in the area.[302] In San Francisco on May 15, he loaded up on avante garde poetry at City Lights bookshop and had dinner with its poet-owner and friend by correspondence, Lawrence Ferlinghetti. Heading back east, he stopped in New Mexico to visit Christ of the Desert Monastery in a remote canyon near Abiquiu, New Mexico. The community of three included one hermit. The monks gave him a Navajo rug for his hermitage chapel. After only twelve days away from Gethsemani, Merton found

himself homesick. He was back home May 21.

News arrived a few days later of the sentencing of Merton's friend Dan Berrigan, along with his brother Phil and seven others, for burning several boxes of draft records in Catonsville, Maryland. The judge ordered the nine imprisoned for six years. While incendiary methods of protest didn't attract Merton, his heart was with those making such symbolic gestures. Once again Merton considered what the war in Vietnam might yet require in his own life. "*Six years! . . . how long will I myself be out of jail? I suppose I can say 'as long as I don't make a special effort to get in'—which is what they did. All I can say is that I haven't deliberately broken any laws. But one of these days I may find myself in a position where I will have to.*"[303]

America seemed to be a shooting gallery. Martin Luther King had been killed. Louisville was among

*"I am on the side of the people who are being burned, cut to pieces, tortured, held as hostages, gassed, ruined, destroyed. They are the victims of both sides. To take sides with massive power is to take sides against the innocent. The side I take is then the side of the people who are sick of war and want peace in order to rebuild their country."*

(Faith and Violence)

[195]

the cities lit up by racial riots. Farm workers trying to organize a union were being jailed and beaten on the fields in California. On June 5 Robert F. Kennedy was killed in Los Angeles. The publication in July of Merton's essays on nonviolence and peacemaking, *Faith and Violence*, was timely.

On June 24, starting to prepare for the Asia trip, Merton went to Louisville to get information for inoculations and visas. He continued to be amazed to have an Abbot who shared his enthusiasms and was so willing to cut all leashes. Dom Flavian suggested the possibility of Merton taking responsibility for setting up a small colony of hermits somewhere on the West Coast. "I get a real sense of openness, of going somewhere — at times it is almost incredible," Merton noted in his journal July 5. His prayer life was flourishing.

*"I have been asked to attend two meetings in Asia, one of them a meeting of the Abbots of Catholic Monastic Orders in that area, the other an interfaith meeting with representatives of Asian religions . . . The length of my stay in Asia is indeterminate. Needless to say, this is not anything unusual in the monastic life. I ask your prayers for the success of this undertaking: and of course, please do not believe anything that rumor may add to this simple scenario."*
(*Circular Letter to Friends, Fall 1968*)

Increasingly his thoughts were Asia-centered. A few lines of poetry catch his mood: "O the mountains of Nepal, / And the tigers and the fevers. / And the escaped bandits from all the world. / And the escaped Trappists, lost, forgotten."[304]

Late in July an invitation arrived from an ecumenical group called the Temple of Understanding asking if Merton would speak at a conference in India. Two weeks later Archbishop Joseph Ryan in Anchorage, Alaska, wrote to ask Merton to lead a retreat for contemplative nuns. In both cases Merton was quite willing. In Alaska, Dom Flavian pointed out, he should take time to see if there might be suitable places for hermitages. In India, he could visit Tibetan Buddhists, perhaps even meet the Dalai Lama. On the way there would be return visits to Christ of the Desert in New Mexico and Our Lady of the Redwoods in California, and a stop in Santa Barbara to see his friend Ping Ferry and give a talk at the Center for the Study of Democratic Institutions.

As July ended, Merton felt he was saying goodbye to Gethsemani and perhaps even to America. "In eight weeks I am to leave here. And who knows — I may not come back. Not that I expect anything to go wrong." There was the possibility of finding a hermitage site in California or Alaska and staying there, or perhaps some isolated place in Asia. "Really I don't care one way or another if I never come back." He noted the problem of nearby traffic, guns, dogs barking in the woods, kids on the lake. "If I can find someplace to *disappear* to I will. And if I am to begin a relatively wandering life with no fixed abode, that's all right too."305

Getting ready to leave, in August he went shopping in Louisville with Frank O'Callaghan, buying luggage and a drip-dry suit.

As September began, though still unsure whether he could visit the Dalai Lama, details of the journey were fairly clear. With departure imminent, Merton's feelings about leaving Gethsemani were more ambiguous than they had been a month before. He experienced a renewed attachment to the monastery fields, felt nervous and insecure, had blisters, and suffered more than ever from allergies. He wrote a form letter to be sent to friends revealing that he was shortly leaving for Asia. He stressed that it was a nonpolitical trip, not linked in any way to the war in Vietnam.

On September 9 his recently appointed secretary, Brother Patrick Hart, came up to the hermitage. He had recently returned from Rome with a gift from Pope Paul for the monk-author he much admired: a beautiful bronze cross. Brother Pat was to live in the hermitage while Merton was away. Brother Maurice Flood and Phil Stark, a Jesuit scholastic who was helping with *Monks Pond*, came with him. The three had breakfast together and said goodbye. Merton sent James Laughlin the draft of his long poem, *Geography of Lograire*, though it wasn't finished.

"I hope [in Asia]," he wrote in his journal, "to find something or someone who will help me advance in my own spiritual quest." He had no intention either to return or not return. "I remain a

*I am about to make my home*
*In the bell's summit*
*Set my mind a thousand feet high*
*On the ace of songs*
*In a mood of needles and random lights*
*To purify*
*The quick magnetic sodas of the skin . . .*

*The threat of winter gleams in gray-haired*
    *windows*
*And witty mirrors*
*And fear lies over the sea*

*But birds fly uncorrected across burnt lands*
*The surest home is pointless:*
*We learn by the cables of orioles*

*I am about to build my nest*
*In the misdirected and unpaid express*
*As I walk away from this poem*

*Hiding the ace of freedoms*
                    (Cables to the Ace)

monk of Gethsemani. Whether or not I end my days here, I don't know and perhaps it is not so important. The great thing is to respond perfectly to God's will in this providential opportunity, whatever it may bring."

The next morning Merton met briefly with Dom Flavian, promising he would behave himself and avoid the press. Dom Flavian gave him money for his travels and the old Bond Street wallet originally given to Merton on his eighteenth birthday by Tom Bennett. Ron Seitz, a Louisville poet who taught at Bellarmine, picked Merton up at 10 A.M. and helped with final errands in Louisville: the collection of allergy pills and the purchase of a pair of shoes. After showering at the O'Callaghan house, there was a dinner party. Merton spent the night at St. Bonaventure's Friary on the Bellarmine campus.

In the morning Merton was away on an early flight to Albuquerque, the first stop on the way to Asia.

Below:
Merton with his secretary, Brother Patrick Hart, on the day of his departure for his Asian journey. (Photograph by Brother Maurice Flood, courtesy of the Abbey of Gethsemani)

*"Our real journey in life is interior; it is a matter of growth, deepening, and of an ever greater surrender to the creative action of love and grace in our hearts. Never was it more necessary for us to respond to that action."*
(Circular Letter to Friends, September 1968)

# Everything Is Compassion

*Yin-yang palace of opposites in unity!*[306]

Merton's stay in New Mexico centered on attending a two-day Indian celebration of the Feast of the Tabernacles, an event closed to the public. Merton was allowed to witness and even photograph the event because he was a "holy man." He flew to Chicago September 16 to give a conference to the Poor Clares, then two days later went on to Alaska to lead a retreat for nuns at the Convent of the Precious Blood. The bishop had arranged for Merton to be taken to possible hermitage sites.

On September 27, travelling by bush plane, he reached Yakutat, a village of Tlingit Indians. The nearby Eyak Lake especially appealed to him. It was silent, surrounded by mountains and populated mainly by thousands of wild geese. Merton could imagine living in such a place, he wrote Dom Flavian, but realized that the key issue to be settled in his life wasn't the postal address. "The important thing for me," he wrote his Abbot, "is not acquiring land or finding an ideal solitude but opening up the depths of my own heart. The rest is secondary."[307]

Waiting at the airport to meet Merton when he arrived in San Francisco October 2 was his young correspondent Suzanne Butorovich and her family. Merton had dinner with them, then stayed the night in a hotel, catching a morning flight to Santa Barbara where Ping Ferry was waiting. A postcard to Dom Flavian sent a few days later showed a view of a bright pink room with king-sized bed at a local

*"May I not come back without having settled the great affair. And found also the great compassion, mahakaruna . . . I am going home, to the home where I have never been in this body . . ."*

(The Asian Journal)

[199]

hotel: "No!" Merton wrote on the back, "I did NOT sleep here!"

Ping Ferry had arranged a talk and discussion at the Center for the Study of Democratic Institutions, a well-endowed establishment for dialogue and research that was slightly to the left. In his exchange with the resident fellows, Merton was critical of the tendency of radical Christians to move toward a "revolutionary mystique," considering everything else irrelevant. His own commitment was to go further with the examination of tradition "because I happen to have an opening towards it, I happen to have the background to do it. . . . A man can only do one thing at a time, and this is the thing that I think I should do." He dismissed forms of renewal that were more concerned with improving breakfast than in "recovering the depths of purpose."[308]

After his several days in Santa Barbara, he drove up the coast with Ping. "How was Merton when you last saw him?" I asked Ping that December. "He was like a kid going to the circus," he replied.

On October 9 Merton arrived at Our Lady of the Redwoods for three days of conferences. The second visit made him certain that the California coast wasn't the right place for a hermitage — there was a land boom in progress and bulldozers everywhere.

Six days later Merton was over the Pacific writing in his journal, "May I not come back without having settled the great affair. And found also the great compassion, *mahakaruna*."[309]

After changing planes in Tokyo, Merton arrived in Bangkok October 16 for a two-day stay. He felt assaulted by the city's wild, filthy streets crowded with motorbikes and buses, though the people were "lovely, beautiful, gentle — except those who are learning too fast from the Americans."[310] Away from the city's noisy center, he found his way to Phra Khantipalo, an English Buddhist monk, who proved sensible despite having "the look of a strict observer." They discussed the Satipatthana Sutra —

*"Before I grasped Zen, the mountains were nothing but mountains and the rivers nothing but rivers. When I got into Zen, the mountains were no longer mountains and the rivers no longer rivers. But when I understood Zen, the mountains were only mountains and the rivers only rivers."*
(Zen saying, Zen and the Birds of Appetite)

the Buddha's Discourse on Mindfulness.[311]

After saying Mass at the local cathedral, Merton got out into the countryside to visit one of the oldest Buddhist shrines, Phra Pathom Chedi.

On October 18 he arrived in Calcutta for the "Spiritual Summit Conference" of the Temple of Understanding, but the topic of ecumenical dialogue was immediately driven from his thoughts by proximity to absolute poverty: technically a monk vowed to poverty, here he was simply a rich American among the destitute, ashamed of the money in his pocket and the camera around his neck. He hardly dared open his mouth until he found Amiya Chakravarty, the scholar to whom Merton had dedicated *Zen and the Birds of Appetite*. He also met an exiled Tibetan lama, Chogyam Trungpa Rimpoche, whose stories of escaping before the Chinese Red Army so impressed Merton that they were to become part of the lecture he gave just before his death.

Perhaps Calcutta, in which penitential life was normal for so many, made Merton regret having left the monastery without asking forgiveness from Dom James, now living as a hermit in a trailer. On October 20 Merton wrote to assure his old Abbot that he had "never personally resented" any of his restrictive decisions "because I knew you were following your conscience and the policies that seemed necessary then."

*"Heartrending routine of the beggars — the little girl who suddenly appeared at the window of the taxi, the utterly lovely smile with which she stretched out her hand and then the extinguishing of the light when she drew it back empty. (I had no Indian money yet.) She fell away from the taxi as if she were sinking in water and drowning and I wanted to die."*
(The Asian Journal)

Speaking at the Calcutta conference October 23, Merton defended all those who are intentionally irrelevant, including those offering monastic witness. He regretted the current upheaval in monasticism that was resulting in "much that is of undying value ... being thrown away irresponsibly" and hoped the situation in the East was better. "I will say as a brother from the West to Eastern monks, be a little careful. ... Your fidelity to tradition will stand you in good stead. Do not be afraid of that fidelity."

In a conference bursting at the seams with talk of convergence and religious oneness, Merton stressed that unity will not be achieved at the level of discourse. "The deepest level of communication is not communication, but communion. It is wordless. It is beyond words, and it is beyond speech, and it is beyond concept. Not that we discover a new unity. We discover an older unity. My dear brothers, we are already one. But we imagine that we are not. What we have to recover is our original unity. What we have to be is what we are."[312]

The next day brought a telegram with the news that Merton was invited to Dharamsala, the residence of the Dalai Lama.

Arriving in New Delhi October 27, Merton was met by Harold Talbott, an American student of Buddhism with whom he corresponded. Talbott was under instruction with the Dalai Lama. They went together to see Tibetan *tankas* (Tibetan icons), then visited with the local Tibetan refugee community. Merton was delighted with Tibetan laughter. He was dazzled by the way they rallied every conceivable sound to make, as it seemed to him, clamorous icons. "The deep sounds renew life, repel the death-grin (i.e., ignorance). The sound is the sound of emptiness. It is profound and clean. We are washed in the millennial silent roar of a rock-eating glacier."[313]

With Talbott on the night train north to Pathankot October 31, Merton was reminded of his momentous train trip to Kentucky in 1941. The next day, winding their way into the Himalayas by a jeep, they reached Talbott's cottage in high up Dharamsala. Ignoring the rain, Merton went off to explore the "beautiful silence" and came upon Tibetans praying with rosaries. The sound of a goatherd's flute floated up from a pasture in the valley a couple of thousand feet below. Yet here too the world of violence made its noises: he could hear the crack of shots from an Indian army small-arms range in the distance, just as he could hear the cannons at Fort Knox at his hermitage at Gethsemani.

The next day one of the Tibetan lamas, Sonbam

> *"Thinking about my own life and future, it is still a very open question. I am beginning to appreciate the hermitage at Gethsemani more than I did last summer when things seemed so noisy and crowded."*
>
> (The Asian Journal)

*"The Dalai Lama is strong and alert, bigger than I expected . . . and very solid, energetic, generous and warm . . . He is a very consecutive thinker and moves from step to step. His ideas on the interior life are built on very solid foundations."*
(The Asian Journal)

Kazi, taught Merton the use of the *mandala* as a method of inner control while meditating and explained the Dzogchen Way (the Great Way of All-Inclusiveness). Merton was delighted to learn that *Trapas* (the closest sound to Trappist) was the Tibetan word for monk.

At Merton's first meeting with the Dalai Lama, November 4, they talked about illusions, misconceptions, metaphysics, and the ideal course of study. Originally only one meeting had been planned, but the Dalai Lama suggested they come together again in two days. Merton was impressed with the Dalai Lama: "a most impressive person . . . strong and alert, bigger than I expected . . . very solid, energetic, generous, and warm . . . charismatic."[314]

There were two mild earthquakes the next day. He thought of the election underway in the United States. That night he dreamed he was back at Gethsemani, not in his Trappist robes but wearing a Zen habit enriched with Tibetan colors, the black joined by red and gold.[315]

Another dream took him to the south of France,

[203]

his original home. At their November 6 meeting, Merton and the Dalai Lama talked about theories of knowledge and compared methods of concentration. Merton said it was important for monks in the world "to be living examples of the freedom and transformation of consciousness which meditation can give." The lamas, he knew, opposed absolute solitude, stressing compassion. Solitude should provide a base for engagement. They talked about methods of concentration and the riddle of the mind concentrating on the mind, while at another level the mind is aware of mind concentrating on mind: "All three one mind." It was a lively conversation. The Dalai Lama "insists on detachment, on an 'unworldly life,' yet sees it as a way to complete understanding of, and participation in, the problems of life and the world." Merton was impressed with the Dalai Lama's step-by-step way of exploring a subject. They agreed to have one more meeting in two days.[316]

The next day he wrote in his journal that contemplative life should open the way to experiencing *temps vierge* — "virginal time": not time as simply a blank sheet to be filled or a territory to be conquered and dominated but time illuminated by compassion.[317] A conversation later in the day with Chobgye Thicchen Rimpoche, a former prisoner of the Chinese, centered on love and compassion. The ideal model of holiness, he said, was not the king (who first of all saves himself) or the boatman (who ferries people to salvation, arriving with them) but the shepherd who goes behind the others, deferring salvation until those he serves have achieved it.

At their third meeting the Dalai Lama wanted to understand the place of vows in a monk's life and what methods Western monks used to free the mind from the rule of passions. What was the reason for avoiding meat? Did they drink alcohol? Or see movies? Merton asked a question about Marxism and monasticism, the subject he planned to discuss at the Bangkok meeting. Was there a connection

*"I do not think I ought to separate myself completely from Gethsemani, even while maintaining an official residence there, legally only. I suppose I ought eventually to end my days there. I do in many ways miss it. There is no problem of my wanting simply to 'leave Gethsemani.' It is my monastery and being away has helped me see it in perspective and love it more."*

(The Asian Journal)

between the Buddhist dialectic and the Marxist concept of alienation? What kind of dialogue was possible between monk and Marxist? The Dalai Lama said that dialogue would be possible between the believer and the Marxist only "if Marxism meant only the establishment of an equitable economic and social structure" and if religious leaders were not servants of secular structures. In actual practice militant atheists seemed unable to make any accommodations and simply struggled to "suppress all forms of religion, good and bad." Merton was impressed by the Dalai Lama's lack of bitterness toward Communists. "I have seldom met anyone with whom I clicked so well," Merton wrote to Dom Flavian.[318]

There were meetings with other Tibetan monks as well, each with his own small house somewhere on the mountain. "What was for me on Friday a rugged, nondescript mountain with a lot of miscellaneous dwellings, rocks, woods, farms, flocks, gulfs, falls, and heights, is now spiritually ordered by permanent seated presences, burning with a lamp-like continuity and significance, centers of awareness and reminders of *dharma*. . . . The central presence is a fully awake, energetic, alert, non-dusty, non-dim, non-whispering Buddha."[319]

After the days at Dharamsala, Merton and Talbott spent a weekend in New Delhi. After exploring an eighteenth-century observatory, Jantar Mantar, they met a Cambodian monk, then visited a Moslem college. Merton said Mass at a local Catholic hospital and worked on his impending Bangkok lecture. Money was running low. "The cost of stamps is breaking me!"

When Merton returned to Calcutta, he had been in India long enough to see not only the destitution but the beauty. He was sensitive to a certain nobility in the city's sordidness. He noticed ponds and lotuses, Communist slogans painted on walls, water buffalo and sacred cows, rickshaws and movie posters, but couldn't find his old friend Bramachari's ashram. The city seemed, if not colorful, more colorful than he had perceived the first time. The urban noise had become a kind of silence. "For the masses of Calcutta, you dimly begin to think, there is no judgment. Only their misery. And instead of being judged, they are a judgment on the rest of the world."[320]

On November 12 Merton and Talbott flew to Darjeeling, the tea district tucked between Nepal, Sikkim, and Bhutan in India's high country. Making the Windamere Hotel his home, he treated a cold he had acquired with tea, shocked at local prices for Western medicine. Though not well, the next day he said Mass at the Loreto Convent, and the day after went looking for Tibetan refugees, finding them scratching out a living in carpet factories or local workshops, but still carrying on the vital religious life which had caused their exile.

On November 16 Merton met Chatral Rimpoche, a lama who looked like a solid old peasant and who proved to be the greatest *rimpoche*[321] Merton had met so far. They talked for two hours with complete understanding of each other as people "on the edge of great realization." Chatral Rimpoche said Merton was a "natural Buddha." He was amazed to find himself so fully at home with a Christian. There was much laughter. "If I were to settle down with a Tibetan guru," Merton noted, "I think Chatral would be the one I'd choose." Before parting they promised each other that they would try to attain complete realization in this life.[322]

For four days Merton rested in a quiet bungalow at the Mim Tea Estate. He wondered if he had yet found "the real Asia." He was still struggling with the question of where he ought to settle down at the end of the pilgrimage. He had the feeling that he ought to end his days at Gethsemani. A "well-behaved, nonviolent Himalayan bee" landed on him several times without stinging. Merton let the bee crawl on his head, collecting sweat "for some electric and gentle honeycomb."

*"The unspoken or half-spoken message of the talk [with Chatral Rimpoche] was our complete understanding of each other as people who were somehow on the edge of great realization and knew it and were trying (somehow or other) to go out and get lost in it—and that it was a grace for us to meet one another . . ."*
(The Asian Journal)

In the distance was one of the great mountains of the Himalayas, Kanchenjunga, which at first annoyed Merton as "a 28,000-foot postcard." But within a few days he realized the mountain had a side not seen in postcards, a hidden mountain that was "a yin-yang palace of opposites in unity." The hidden mountain cannot be photographed. Its full beauty "is not seen until you consent to the impossible paradox" of knowing that the mountain both is and is not. "When nothing more needs to be said, the smoke of ideas clears, the mountain is SEEN."[323]

Back in Darjeeling on November 21, Merton said Mass at the Loreto Convent, then gave a talk voicing his reservations about the renewal going on in the West. "We need the religious genius of Asia and Asian culture to inject a fresh dimension of depth into our aimless threshing about. I would almost say an element of heart, of *bhakti*, of love."[324] He met Karlu Rimpoche, who lived at the hermit center at Sonada, the most soft-spoken lama Merton had yet encountered. They talked at length about the hermit life: who can live it, the spiritual life at its center, the appropriate methods and subjects of meditation, the schedule to be followed. The lama told Merton that he possessed the "true Mahayana spirit."[325] (Mahayana—literally, Great Vehicle—is the branch of Buddhism that gives particular stress to compassion and universal salvation.)

Above:
A Buddhist shrine, photographed by Merton in Sri Lanka. (Courtesy of the Merton Legacy Trust)

Travelling back to Calcutta, Merton happened to meet a man named John Balfour, who years later still recalled the encounter. Balfour was impressed at Merton's halo-like, cleaner-than-clean, "washed" face, the kind of face that usually belongs to those in "some major mystic dimension."[326]

When Merton returned once again to Calcutta, it had become "a city I love." There were still the disintegrating slums, yet Calcutta had become more colorful, graced with white cranes and green coconut palms. It was a very brief stay this time. Then Merton was on to Madras in the south of India.

On November 27 he visited the Cathedral of St. Thomas, his namesake, the apostle who came all the way to Asia and died there. Afterward he said the Mass of Saint Thomas at the Church of Our Lady of Expectation on St. Thomas Mount, then visited a crèche for abandoned children next door. There was a *lingam* (a phallic symbol) of black stone standing in the ocean near the shore, washed by wave after wave, an image of man and woman. The next day he went to the temple complex of Mahabalipuram, a Hindu shrine on the coast covered with bas-reliefs of handsome gods and shapely goddesses. Merton had a sense of ancient India before the British Raj.

Arriving in Colombo, Sri Lanka, on November 29, Merton found himself in the midst of strikes, with police and soldiers everywhere. After checking into the Hotel Karma, he went to the United States Information Agency, hoping to get assistance in making contact with local Buddhist scholars. The

Below:
While in Sri Lanka, Merton photographed this statue of the Sleeping Buddha. (Photograph courtesy of the Merton Legacy Trust)

*"I am able to approach the Buddhas barefoot and undisturbed, my feet in wet grass, wet sand. Then the silence of the extraordinary faces. The great smiles. Huge and yet subtle. Filled with every possibility, questioning nothing, knowing everything, rejecting nothing, the peace not of emotional resignation but of Madhyamika, of sunyata, that has seen through every question without trying to discredit anyone or anything— without refutation—without establishing some other argument. For the doctrinaire, the mind that needs well-established positions, such peace, such silence, can be frightening."*

(The Asian Journal)

director turned out to be a great fan of Merton's, Victor Stier, who at the time was reading *Conjectures of a Guilty Bystander*.

Early the next day Merton was off by train to the center of Sri Lanka, riding second class on the Kandy Express in a compartment reserved for clergy, checking into a hotel in Kandy with a view of a church so English that, were it not for the coconut palms, it might have been in Sussex. He set off to find the *bhikkhu* (monk, from the Sanskrit word for beggar) Nyanaponika Thera at his monastery in the jungle not far from the city. They walked to a nearby temple. What impressed Merton most was an old Buddha statue carved out of a rock rising out of the earth.

The climax of Merton's visit to Sri Lanka, and one of the significant moments in his life, came when he visited Polonnaruwa on December 3. Polonnaruwa, an ancient ruined city in the northeast of Sri Lanka, is a place of pilgrimage known mainly for its colossal figures of the Buddha carved out of huge stones. Perhaps most impressive is the vast sculpture of the sleeping/dying Buddha. Merton was so stunned by what he experienced in the presence of the carvings that it was three days before he attempted writing about it. He had been able to wander among the huge figures alone. The priest who had driven him there, alarmed at such proximity to paganism, stayed in the car.

> I was suddenly, almost forcibly, jerked clean
> out of the habitual, half-tied vision of things,
> and an inner cleanness, clarity, as if exploding
> from the rocks themselves, became evident,
> obvious. The queer *evidence* of the reclining fig-
> ure, the smile, and the sad smile of Ananda,
> standing with arms folded (much more "imper-
> ative" than Da Vinci's Mona Lisa because it
> was completely simple and straightforward).
> The thing about all this is that there is no puz-
> zle, no problem, and really no "mystery." All

problems are resolved and everything is clear, simply because what matters is clear. The rock, all matter, all life, is charged with *Dharmakaya* [Buddha-nature, Buddha meaning anyone fully awake, fully in touch with reality and free of all illusion] . . . everything is emptiness and everything is compassion. I don't know when in my life I have ever had such a sense of beauty and spiritual validity running together in one aesthetic illumination. Surely, with Mahabalipuram and Polonnaruwa, my Asian pilgrimage has come clear and purified itself—I mean I know and have seen what I was obscurely looking for. I don't know what else remains but I have now seen and have pierced through the surface and have got beyond the shadow and the disguise. This is Asia in its purity, not covered over with garbage (Asian or European or American) and it is clear, pure, complete. It says everything—it needs nothing. And because it needs nothing it can afford to be silent, unnoticed, undiscovered. It does not need to be discovered. It is we (Asians included) who need to discover it.[327]

Below:
Thomas Merton (center) sits among other participants in the Bangkok conference of Benedictine and Trappist Abbots, on the day of his death. Beside Merton (second from the left) is Jean Leclerq, O.S.B. (Photograph by Dom Cees Tholens, O.S.B., courtesy of Boston College, Burns Library).

# Jonas Overshadowed

*We can ask ourselves if we are planning for the next twenty years to be travelling with a train of yaks.*

Merton stopped in Singapore December 4, staying at the Raffles Hotel. He booked a flight to Djakarta for December 15, his intended next stop after the conference of abbots and abbesses. He planned to spend Christmas at Rawa Seneng (Peaceful Swamp), a Trappist monastery on Java. From there he would proceed to Hong Kong to stay with the Trappists on Lantao Island.

Merton returned to Bangkok December 6. Just as Calcutta had changed each time he came back to it, Bangkok too was different; overwhelmed the first time by noise and dirt, now he was impressed by playing children and the plenitude of fruit, rice, meat, bottles, medicines, shoes, machinery, lights, and trinkets. Merton went to the fabulous Temple of the Emerald Buddha, magnificent, bizarre, and slightly flattened by the feet and flash bulbs of so many tourists. "There are of course Disneyland tendencies in all these Thai wats," Merton noted. "And I suppose at times they go over the line."[328]

On December 8, the Feast of the Immaculate Conception, Merton made his last journal entry. He was off to say Mass at the Church of St. Louis, then to have lunch at the Apostolic Delegation before going to the Sawang Kaniwat (Red Cross) Conference Center.

The meeting place was at Samutprakan, 29 miles

*"Abbot Lot came to Abbot Joseph and said: Father, according as I am able, I keep my little rule, and my little fast, my prayer, meditation and contemplative silence; and according as I am able to strive to cleanse my heart of thoughts: now what more should I do? The elder rose up in reply and stretched out his hands to heaven, and his fingers became like ten lamps of fire. He said: Why not be totally changed into fire?"*
(The Wisdom of the Desert)

south of Bangkok. Merton arrived in the afternoon and was housed on the ground floor of Cottage Two.

The conference began the next day with a welcoming address from the Supreme Patriarch of Thai Buddhism. Events of the day included an evening discussion on marriage and celibacy.

Few of the monks got much sleep that night. A chorus of cats had come out to sing the night office on nearby roofs; following crescendos of cat howling, those in adjacent rooms heard Merton's laughter.[329]

Merton's paper, "Marxism and Monastic Perspectives," so much on his mind for many weeks, was presented the next morning. Merton, under orders from his abbot to avoid the press, was made nervous by a Dutch television crew which had turned up to film his lecture.

One of the crucial issues confronting the monk, Merton pointed out, is what his position is and how he identifies himself in a world of revolution. This wasn't simply a matter of how to survive an enemy who is intent on either destroying or converting those of religious convictions. Rather, it is a matter of understanding, beyond present models of Marxism and monasticism, fundamental points of similarity and difference.

He recognized significant similarities. The monk, after all, "is essentially someone who takes up a critical attitude toward the world and its structures . . . [saying] that the claims of the world are fraudulent." In addition, both monk and Marxist share the idea that each should give according to his capacity and receive according to his need. But while the Marxist gives primary emphasis to the material and economic structures of life, seeing religious approaches as mystification, the monk is committed to bringing about a human transformation that begins at the level of consciousness.

"Instead of starting with matter itself and then moving up to a new structure, in which man will

Above:
Merton in Bangkok delivering his talk on Marxism and Monastic Perspectives, hours before his death. (Photograph courtesy of the Abbey of Gethsemani)

*"This, I think, is what Buddhism is all about, and what Christianity is about, what monasticism is about—if you understand it in terms of grace . . . We can no longer rely on being supported by structures that may be destroyed at any moment . . . The Zen people have a saying: . . . 'Where do you go from the top of a thirty-foot pole?' "*
*(From Merton's last talk, The Asian Journal)*

[212]

automatically develop a new consciousness, the traditional religions begin with the consciousness of the individual seeking to transform and liberate the truth in each person, with the idea that it will then communicate itself to others." This is emphatically the vocation of the monk "who seeks full realization ... [and] has come to experience the ground of his own being in such a way that he knows the secret of liberation and can somehow or other communicate it to others." At the deepest level, the monk is teaching others how to live by love. For Christians, this is the discovery of Christ dwelling in all others.

Only with such love, Merton went on, is it possible to realize the economic ideal of each giving according to his ability and receiving according to his need. But in actuality many Christians, including those in monastic communities, have not reached this level of love and realization. They have burdened their lives with too many false needs and these have blocked the way to full realization, the monk's only reason for being.

Merton told a story he had heard from Chogyam Trungpa Rimpoche of a Buddhist abbot fleeing from his Tibetan monastery before the advance of Chinese Communist troops. Another monk joined him with a train of twenty-five yaks loaded with the treasures of the monastery and "essential" provisions. The abbot didn't stay with the treasure or the treasurer; travelling light, he at last reached India, destitute but alive. The yak-tending monk, unable to leave valuables behind, was overtaken by the soldiers and was never heard of again.

"We can ask ourselves," Merton said, "if we are planning for the next twenty years to be travelling with a train of yaks." Monasticism, after all, is not architecture or clothing or even rules of life. It is "total inner transformation. Let the yaks take care of themselves." The monastic life thrives whenever there is a person "giving some kind of direction and instruction to a small group attempting to love God and reach union with him."

"The monk belongs to the world, but the world belongs to him, insofar as he has dedicated himself totally to liberation from it in order to liberate it. You can't just immerse yourself in the world and get carried away with it. That is no salvation. If you want to pull a drowning man out of the water, you have to have some support yourself."

(The Asian Journal)

[213]

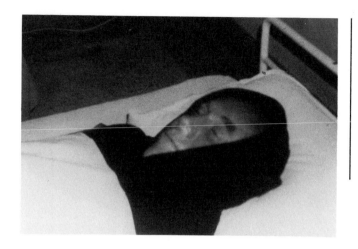

This kind of monasticism cannot be extinguished. "It is imperishable. It represents an instinct of the human heart, and it represents a charism given by God to man. It cannot be rooted out, because it does not depend on man. It does not depend on cultural factors, and it does not depend on sociological or psychological factors. It is something much deeper."[330]

Finishing the talk, Merton suggested putting off questions until the evening session. He concluded with the words, "So I will disappear." He suggested everyone have a Coke.

At about 3 P.M. Father François de Grunne, who had a room near Merton's, heard a cry and what sounded like someone falling. He knocked on Merton's door but there was no response. Shortly before 4 o'clock Father de Grunne came down again to get the cottage key from Merton and to reassure himself that nothing was the matter. When there was no answer he looked through the louvers in the upper part of the door and saw Merton lying on the terrazzo floor. A standing fan had fallen on top of him. Father de Grunne tried to open the door but it was locked. With the help of others, the door was opened.

There was a smell of burned flesh. Merton, clearly

dead, was lying on his back with the five-foot fan diagonally across his body. Dom Odo Haas, Abbot of Waekwan, tried to lift it and received an electric shock that jerked him sideways, holding him fast to the shaft of the fan until Father Celestine Say pulled the plug.

A long, raw third-degree burn about a hand's width ran along the right side of Merton's body almost to the groin. There were no marks on his hands. His face was bluish-red, eyes and mouth half open. There had been bleeding from the back of the head. The priests gave Merton absolution, then Dom Odo went to get the Abbot Primate of the Benedictines, Dom Rembert Weakland, who gave Merton extreme unction. A doctor arrived, Mother Edeltrud Weist, Prioress of Taegu Convent in Korea. She checked for pulse and eye reaction to light.

A police test of the fan showed that a "defective electric cord was installed inside its stand. . . . The flow of electricity was strong enough to cause the death of a person if he touched the metal part." After Merton's body was released to Dom Weakland, it was washed, then taken to the chapel. There was a prayer vigil throughout the night at the side of the body.

The next day Merton's body was taken to the United States Air Force Base in Bangkok and from there flown back to the United States in company with dead bodies of Americans killed in Vietnam. From Oakland, California, it continued by civilian carrier, reaching the Abbey of Gethsemani December 17. The casket was opened briefly; several monks identified the body.

The funeral Mass was composed by Father Chrysogonus Waddell. On the cover of the Liturgy booklet was a text from *The Sign of Jonas*: "I have always overshadowed Jonas with My Mercy. . . . Have you lost sight of me Jonas My Child? Mercy within mercy within mercy."

At the end of the Mass, there was a reading from

Below:
The funeral Mass for Thomas Merton was held in the renovated Abbey Church at Gethsemani. (Photograph courtesy of the Abbey of Gethsemani)

*"The world knew him from his books: we knew him from his spoken word. Few, if any, knew him in his secret prayer. Still, he had a secret prayer, and this is what gave the inner life to all he said and wrote. His secret was his secret to himself to a great extent, but he was a skillful reader of the secret of the souls that sought his help. It is because of this that although we laughed at him, and with him, as we would a younger brother, still we respected him as the spiritual father of our souls."*
(Dom Flavian Burns, Abbot of Gethsemani, in a homily to the monastery community)

[215]

*The Seven Storey Mountain*, concluding with the book's prophetic final sentence, "That you may become the brother of God and learn to know the Christ of the burnt men."

His brother monks buried Merton in their small cemetery next to the abbey church.

With the body came an official declaration of Merton's effects, appraised in dollars:

| | |
|---|---|
| 1 Timex Watch | $10.00 |
| 1 Pair Dark Glasses in Tortoise Frames | Nil |
| 1 Cistercian Leather Bound Breviary | Nil |
| 1 Rosary (broken) | Nil |
| 1 Small Icon on Wood of Virgin and Child | Nil |

There was the memory of Merton's last words. After the morning conference, Father de Grunne told Merton that a nun in the audience was annoyed that Merton had said nothing about converting people.

"What we are asked to do at present," Merton responded, "is not so much to speak of Christ as to let him live in us so that people may find him by feeling how he lives in us."

The icon Merton had with him contains its own last words, silent on one side, and in the form of a text in Merton's hand on the back:

If we wish to please the true God and to be friends with the most blessed of friendships, let us present our spirit naked to God. Let us not draw into it anything of this present world—no art, no thought, no reasoning, no self-justification—even though we should possess all the wisdom of this world.[331]

Below:
Thomas Merton's grave at the Abbey of Gethsemani. (Photograph courtesy of Tommie O'Callaghan)

*"I will give you what you desire. I will lead you into solitude. I will lead you by the way that you cannot possibly understand, because I want it to be the quickest way . . .*

*"Everything that touches you shall burn you, and you will draw your hand away in pain, until you have withdrawn yourself from all things. Then you will be all alone . . .*

*"Do not ask when it will be or where it will be or how it will be: On a mountain or in a prison, in a desert or in a concentration camp or in a hospital or at Gethsemani. It does not matter. So do not ask me, because I am not going to tell you. You will not know until you are in it.*

*"But you shall taste the true solitude of my anguish and my poverty and I shall lead you into the high places of my joy and you shall die in Me and find all things in My Mercy which has created you for this end . . .*

*"That you may become the brother of God and learn to know the Christ of the burnt men."*
(The Seven Storey Mountain)

[216]

# Notes

1. Thomas Merton, *The Seven Storey Mountain* (New York: Harcourt Brace, 1948), 7. Hereafter referred to as SSM.

2. SSM, 3.

3. SSM, 11.

4. SSM, 5.

5. Entry of January 2, 1950, Thomas Merton, *The Sign of Jonas* (New York: Harcourt Brace, 1953), 262. Hereafter referred to as SJ.

6. SSM, 8.

7. SSM, 9.

8. SSM, 14.

9. Evelyn Scott, letter to Lola Ridge, January 15, 1926. Reprinted in Michael Mott, *The Seven Mountains of Thomas Merton* (Boston: Houghton Mifflin, 1984), 26. Hereafter referred to as Mott.

10. SSM, 18.

11. SSM, 23.

12. SSM, 36.

13. SSM, 36.

14. SSM, 37.

15. SSM, 56.

16. Mott, 37-38.

17. SSM, 51.

18. Mott, 37.

19. SSM, 51-52.

20. SSM, 54.

21. SSM, 54.

22. SSM, 60.

23. SSM, 61.

24. SSM, 62.

25. SSM, 64-65.

26. SSM, 67.

27. SSM, 73-74.

28. SSM, 79.

29. SSM, 80.

30. Thomas Merton, "A Tribute to Gandhi," *Seeds of Destruction* (New York: Farrar Straus &

Giroux, 1964), 222; idem, *The Nonviolent Alternative* (New York: Farrar Straus & Giroux, 1975), 178.

31. Mott, 60.

32. SSM, 82-83.

33. SSM, 83.

34. SSM, 83.

35. SSM, 85.

36. SSM, 88.

37. SSM, 93.

38. SSM, 103.

39. Thomas Merton, *My Argument with the Gestapo* (New York: Doubleday, 1969), 5. Hereafter referred to as MAG.

40. SSM, 108.

41. SSM, 108.

42. SSM, 109.

43. Letters to June Yungblut, June 22, 1967 and March 29, 1968; reprinted in *The Hidden Ground of Love: The Letters of Thomas Merton on Religious Experience and Social Concerns*, edited by William H. Shannon (New York: Farrar Straus & Giroux, 1985), 637, 642-43. Hereafter referred to as HGL. For further attention to this aspect of Merton, see Donna Kristoff, "Light That Is Not Light: A Consideration of Thomas Merton and the Icon," *The Merton Annual*, volume 2 (New York: AMS Press, 1989), 84-117; and Dom John Eudes Bamberger, "Thomas Merton and the Christian East," *One Yet Two: Monastic Tradition East and West* (Kalamazoo, Michigan: Cistercian Publications, 1976), 440-51.

44. SSM, 110.

45. SSM, 111.

46. SSM, 111.

47. SSM, 113.

48. SSM, 122.

49. SSM, 120.

50. SSM, 122.

51. Mott, 77.

52. SSM, 128.

53. Mott, 78.

54. Mott, 79.

55. Mott, 79.

56. MAG, 138.

57. Thomas Merton, *Collected Poems* (New York: New Directions, 1977), 104.

58. SSM, 124.

59. Letter to the author, undated.

60. SSM, 121.

61. SSM, 124.

62. Restricted Journal, January 30, 1965; Mott, 77.

63. Merton's will on taking simple vows at the Abbey of Gethsemani, Abbey Archives; also see Mott, 90.

64. SSM, 124-25.
65. SSM, 126.
66. SSM, 123.
67. SSM, 127.
68. SSM, 128.
69. MAG, 149.
70. SSM, 133.
71. SSM, 134.
72. SSM, 133.
73. SSM, 139.
74. SSM, 137.
75. SSM, 147.
76. SSM, 148.
77. SSM, 145-46.
78. SSM, 149.
79. SSM, 149.
80. SSM, 153.
81. SSM, 153.
82. SSM, 181, 237.
83. SSM, 159.
84. SSM, 171.
85. SSM, 174.
86. SJ, 362.
87. SSM, 175.
88. May 18, 1941, St. Bonaventure Journal, unpublished.
89. SSM, 185.
90. William Blake, "Poems from the Notebook 1800-1803," *Complete Writings* (Oxford: Oxford University Press, 1969), 418.
91. SSM, 190.
92. William Blake, preface to "Milton: a Poem in 2 Books," ibid, 480.
93. SSM, 203; William Blake, "Augeries of Innocence," ibid, 431-34.
94. SSM, 189, 191.
95. SSM, 196.
96. SSM, 196.
97. SSM, 198.
98. SSM, 201.
99. SSM, 200.
100. Published posthumously; Thomas Merton, *The Literary Essays of Thomas Merton* (New York: New Directions, 1981), 387-453.
101. SSM, 204.
102. SSM, 206.
103. SSM, 207.
104. SSM, 210-11.
105. SSM, 205.

106. SSM, 214.

107. SSM, 215-16.

108. SSM, 216.

109. Mott, 120-21.

110. SSM, 224-25.

111. SSM, 235.

112. SSM, 236.

113. SSM, 237-38.

114. SSM, 241.

115. SSM, 248.

116. SSM, 250.

117. SSM, 255.

118. SSM, 220.

119. SSM, 259.

120. SSM, 264.

121. SSM, 279.

122. Thomas Merton, *The Secular Journal of Thomas Merton* (New York: Farrar Straus & Cudahy, 1958), 75-78.

123. SSM, 284-85.

124. SSM, 292-93.

125. SSM, 296.

126. SSM, 298.

127. SSM, 301.

128. SSM, 305-6.

129. SSM, 308.

130. SSM, 301; there is a specific reference in an unpublished journal entry dated January 30, 1965; also see Mott, 162.

131. *Secular Journal*, 110.

132. MAG, 21.

133. MAG, 26-28.

134. MAG, 76-77.

135. MAG, 160-61.

136. St. Bonaventure Journal, March 4, 1941.

137. SSM, 311-12.

138. *Secular Journal*, 267.

139. *Secular Journal*, 183.

140. *Secular Journal*, 203.

141. St. Bonaventure Journal, August 4, 1941.

142. SSM, 345.

143. SSM, 345.

144. SSM, 348.

145. Letter to Mark Van Doren, November 28, 1941; *The Road to Joy: Letters to New and Old Friends*, ed. Robert E. Daggy (New York: Farrar Straus & Giroux, 1989), 13. Hereafter referred to as Road.

146. *Secular Journal*, 269.

147. HGL, 10.

148. Letter to Bob Lax, December 6, 1941; Road, 163.

149. Road, 15.

150. Road, 164-67.

151. SSM, 398.

152. SSM, 404.

153. SJ, 18.

154. SSM, 410.

155. Letter to James Laughlin, March 1, 1945; see Mott, 226.

156. Chrysogonus Waddell, *The Merton Annual*, volume 2, 1989, 69.

157. See Mott, 227.

158. Robert Giroux, in *Merton by Those Who Knew Him Best*, ed. Paul Wilkes (New York: Harper & Row, 1984), 20.

159. SJ, 110.

160. Robert Giroux, in *Merton by Those Who Knew Him Best*, 20.

161. SJ, 109.

162. SJ, 165.

163. SJ, 14.

164. SJ, 72.

165. SJ, 59.

166. SJ, 41.

167. SJ, 154.

168. SJ, 89.

169. SJ, 22.

170. SJ, 28.

171. SJ, 60.

172. SJ, 95, 97.

173. SJ, 113.

174. SJ, 120.

175. SJ, 157.

176. SJ, 125.

177. SJ, 151-52.

178. SJ, 170.

179. SJ, 186.

180. Road, 193.

181. Road, 23.

182. SJ, 193.

183. SJ, 207.

184. SJ, 269.

185. Journal, March 30, 1957.

186. SJ, 251-52.

187. SJ, 273.

188. Conversation with the author.

189. SJ, 328.

190. SJ, 322.

191. SJ, 334.

192. SJ, 337.

193. SJ, 338-39.

194. SJ, 340-41.

195. SJ, 275.

196. SJ, 11.

197. Thomas Merton, *The Silent Life* (New York: Farrar Straus & Cudahy, 1957), 153-54.

198. Journal, October 10, 1952.

199. Journal, October 22, 1952.

200. Journal, December 20, 1959.

201. For a more detailed account of the Merton-Zilboorg meeting and its aftermath, see Mott, 290-99.

202. Mott, 296-97.

203. Mott, 298.

204. Thomas Merton, *Conjectures of a Guilty Bystander* (New York: Doubleday & Co., 1966), 12; for the text of the original journal entry, see Mott, 306.

205. Boris Pasternak and Thomas Merton, *Six Letters*, intro. Lydia Pasternak Slater (Lexington, Kentucky: The King Library Press, 1973). Also see Thomas Merton, "The Pasternak Affair," *Disputed Questions* (New York: Farrar Straus & Cudahy, 1960); and *The Literary Essays of Thomas Merton*.

206. *Six Letters*, October 23, 1958.

207. *Conjectures of a Guilty Bystander*, 140-42.

208. The comment was made in conversation with the author.

209. HGL, 136-37.

210. Thomas Merton, *No Man Is an Island* (New York: Harcourt Brace, 1955), 138.

211. Journal, December 17, 1959.

212. Mott, 340-41.

213. Journal, May 8, 1960.

214. HGL, 483-84, letter to Pope John dated November 10, 1958; Merton also mentioned his interest in Russia.

215. HGL, 484-85.

216. The stole is on exhibition at the Thomas Merton Study Center at Bellarmine College in Louisville.

217. Journal, October 3, 1960.

218. Journal, December 26, 1960; original text in Latin.

219. Undated letter to Sister Madeleva, included in *Seeds of Destruction* (New York: Farrar Straus & Giroux, 1964), 274-75; for Julian of Norwich's writing, see *Showings* (Ramsey, New Jersey: Paulist Press, 1978).

220. Journal, April 25, 1957.

221. Journal, March 4, 1958.

222. Journal, March 19, 1958.

223. Letter to Victor Hammer, May 14, 1959.

224. Journal, July 2, 1960.

225. Journal, October 29, 1960.

226. "The Nature Who makes nature;" see Saint Thomas Aquinas, *Summa*, I.2, 85 nr 6.

227. *Hagia Sophia* was published in *Emblems of a Season of Fury* (New York: New Directions, 1961), 61-69; and later was included in the revised *Thomas Merton Reader*, ed. T. P. McDonnell (New York: Doubleday-Image, 1974) and *The Collected Poems of Thomas Merton*, 363-71.

228. Thomas Merton, *The Behavior of Titans* (New York: New Directions, 1961), 65-71.

229. Originally published in *The Catholic Worker*; included in *Collected Poems*, 345-49.

230. Published in March 1962 by New Directions and included in *Collected Poems*, 293.

231. Letter to Dorothy Day, July 23, 1961; HGL, 139.

232. Letter to Dorothy Day, August 23, 1961; HGL, 139-40.

233. *The Catholic Worker*, October 1961.

234. Letter to Pope John, November 11, 1961; HGL, 486. Msgr. Capovilla, private secretary to Pope John, recalls that the letter impressed the Pope. "It may have had some influence on the writing of *Pacem in Terris*," says Msgr. William Shannon.

235. Letter to Jim Forest, January 5, 1962; HGL, 261. (Some portions of the letter used here were not reproduced in HGL.)

236. The book was published in September 1962. Merton's name was featured on the cover, not as editor, but rather as author of the introduction.

237. Letter to Jim Forest; HGL, 266-68.

238. Letter to Jim Forest, June 14, 1962; HGL, 268-69.

239. See Mott, 379, and Mott endnote nr. 228, 623.

240. Another book of Merton's never reached the public, not because of censorship but because his publishers thought Merton's views were too old-fashioned. *Art and Worship* was to have been published in 1959. At least one reader of the manuscript, Eloise Spaeth, could not bear Merton's " 'sacred artist' who keeps creeping in with his frightful icons." Unfortunately this book was never put out in a mimeographed edition, though a few chapters were published as magazine articles. For a summary of the still-unpublished book, see Donna Kristoff's essay, "Light That Is Not Light," *The Merton Annual*, volume 2, 1989, 93-97.

241. Bob Grip tells me he came upon a copy of *Peace in the Post-Christian Era* on a window sill in the library of the Vatican's North American College in Rome.

242. Letter to poet and printer John Beecher, July 9, 1963.

243. Letter to Jim Forest, July 7, 1962; HGL, 269.

244. Letter to Jim Forest, April 26, 1963; HGL, 274.

245. Journal, May 10, 1963; Mott, 386.

246. *The Nonviolent Alternative*, "In Acceptance of the Pax Medal, 1963," 257-58.

247. Letter to Dorothy Day, June 16, 1962; HGL, 145.

248. *Seeds of Destruction*, 129.

249. Letter to Jim Forest, January 17, 1963; HGL, 273.

250. Letter to Jim Forest, January 29, 1962; HGL, 261-63.

251. Letter to Jim Forest, January 29, 1962; HGL, 262.

252. Letter to Dorothy Day, December 20, 1961; HGL, 140-43.

253. Letter to Jim Forest, February 6, 1962; HGL, 263-64.

254. Letter to Jim Forest, December 8, 1962; HGL, 272.

255. Letter to Jim Forest, January 29, 1962; HGL, 262.

256. Letter to Jim Forest, February 21, 1966; HGL, 294-97.

257. Thomas Merton, *Gandhi on Nonviolence* (New York: New Directions, 1965), 20.

258. Thomas Merton, *Raids on the Unspeakable* (New York: New Directions, 1966), 45-53.

259. Thomas Merton, *A Vow of Conversation* (New York: Farrar Straus & Giroux, 1988), 32-33.

260. *A Vow of Conversation*, 101.

261. *Raids on the Unspeakable*, 9-23.

262. A paper on the retreat theme by Merton is included in *The Nonviolent Alternative*, 259-60. Also see *Thomas Merton's Struggle with Peacemaking* (Erie, Pa.: St. Benet Press, 1979), 28-30; and Mott, 406-7.

263. *A Vow of Conversation*, 140.

264. *A Vow of Conversation*, 144-45.

265. *A Vow of Conversation*, 193-94.

266. Letter to Jim Forest; HGL, 285.

267. Thomas Merton, cassette tape, *Life and Solitude*, side B, "Hermit's Legacy: Life Without Care" (Electronic Paperbacks).

268. Letter to Bob Lax, October 16, 1965, published in Bob Lax and Thomas Merton, *A Catch of Anti-Letters* (Kansas City, Mo.: Sheed Andrews & McMeel, 1978), 61.

269. Letter to Jim Forest, November 11, 1965; HGL, 285-86.

270. Letter to Jim Forest, November 19, 1965; HGL, 287-88. For a more detailed account of this event in Merton's life see Forest, *Thomas Merton's Struggle with Peacemaking*, and Mott, 427-30.

271. Letter to John Heidbrink, Church Work Secretary of the Fellowship of Reconciliation, December 4, 1965; HGL, 424-26.

272. The essay is included in both *Faith and Violence* (Notre Dame, Ind.: University of Notre Dame Press, 1968) and *The Nonviolent Alternative*.

273. *Faith and Violence*, 27.

274. Letter to Marco Pallis, December 5, 1965; HGL, 473-74.

275. Letter to Abdul Aziz, January 2, 1966; HGL, 62-64.

276. Thomas Merton, "Evening: Long Distance Call," *Eighteen Poems* (New York: New Directions, 1985).

277. To preserve her privacy, I refer to her only as Margie.

278. For a detailed account of this period of Merton's life, see Mott, 435-54 and 461-62, and John Howard Griffin, *Follow the Ecstacy* (Fort Worth, Texas: Latitudes Press, 1983), 77-131. Unless otherwise noted, all the quotations used in this chapter are from these two sources.

279. Mott, 443.

280. "Louisville Airport," *Eighteen Poems*.

281. "Certain Proverbs Arise Out of Dreams," *Eighteen Poems*.

282. "Never Call a Babysitter in a Thunderstorm," *Eighteen Poems*.

283. "Cherokee Park," *Eighteen Poems*.

284. Road, 97.

285. Letter to Bob Lax, January 26, 1967; published *A Catch of Anti-Letters*, 110.

286. Guy Davenport, "The Anthropology of Table Manners," *The Geography of the Imagination* (San Francisco: The North Point Press, 1981), 348.

287. Griffin, 139-40.

288. These are among pieces collected in *The Literary Essays of Thomas Merton*.

289. *Ishi Means Man* (Greensboro, N.C.: Unicorn Press, 1976).

290. Some of Merton's essays on these themes are collected in *Contemplative in a World of Action* (New York: Doubleday, 1971) and *The Monastic Journey* (Kansas City, Mo.: Sheed Andrews & McMeel, 1977).

291. Merton's prefaces for foreign editions of his books are collected in *Honorable Reader* (New York: Crossroad, 1989).

292. The four issues of *Monks Pond* were published in book form by the University of Kentucky Press in 1989.

293. Many of Merton's taped lectures are available on cassette tape, one series produced by Electronic Paperbacks, another by Credence Cassettes. Merton's lecture on the Cargo Cults was transcribed and published in edited form in *Love and Living* (New York: Farrar Straus & Giroux, 1967), 80-94.

294. Road, 308-13.

295. Letter to Jim Forest, June 17, 1967; HGL, 303.

296. December 17, 1967; Griffin, 175.

297. Letter to June Yungblut, November 19, 1967; HGL, 638.

298. Merton's letters to Dom Flavian are included in *School of Charity: The Letters of Thomas Merton on Religious Renewal and Spiritual Direction*, edited by Brother Patrick Hart (New York: Farrar Straus & Giroux, 1990).

299. Letter to D. T. Suzuki, March 12, 1959; *Encounters: Thomas Merton and D.T. Suzuki*, ed. Robert E. Daggy (Lexington, Ky.: Larkspur Press, 1988), 5-6.

300. For Merton's description of their meeting, see *Encounters*, 84-86.

301. Letter to Jean Leclercq, March 9, 1968; *The School of Charity*, 369-70.

302. Thomas Merton, *Woods, Shore, Desert* (Santa Fe: Museum of New Mexico Press, 1982), the journal of Merton's trip to California and New Mexico. Photos from the trip appear in this book as well as in *A Hidden Wholeness* (Boston: Houghton Mifflin, 1970) and *Geography of Holiness* (New York: Pilgrim Press, 1980).

303. Journal, May 28, 1968.

304. Journal, July 19, 1968; Mott, 529.

305. Journal, July 29, 1968; Mott, 532.

306. Thomas Merton, *Asian Journal* (New York: New Directions, 1973), 156.

307. Letter to Dom Flavian Burns, October 9, 1968; *The School of Charity*, 402. For details of Merton's Alaska visit, see *Thomas Merton in Alaska: The Alaskan Conferences, Journals, and Letters*, ed. Robert E. Daggy (New York: New Directions, 1988).

308. *Preview of the Asian Journey*, ed. Walter Capps (New York: Crossroad, 1989), includes the transcript of the formal dialogue with Merton at the Center.

309. *Asian Journal*, 4-5.

310. *Asian Journal*, 13-14.

311. An essay on mindfulness by Bhikkhu Khantipalo is included in *Asian Journal*, 297-304.

312. *Asian Journal*, 307-8, also see 315-17.

313. *Asian Journal*, 68-69.

314. *Asian Journal*, 100-102.

315. *Asian Journal*, 107.

316. *Asian Journal*, 112-13.

317. *Asian Journal*, 117.

318. *Asian Journal*, 178-79.

319. *Asian Journal*, 105-6.

320. *Asian Journal*, 132.

321. *Rimpoche*, Tibetan for "precious one," is used to refer to spiritual masters.

322. *Asian Journal*, 142-45.

323. *Asian Journal*, 156-57.

324. From a tape transcribed by Brother Patrick Hart.

325. *Asian Journal*, 163-66.

326. Letter of John Balfour to Brother Patrick Hart, February 11, 1976; Mott, 555.

327. *Asian Journal*, 233-35.

328. *Asian Journal*, 250.

329. Among various accounts of Merton's last days, the most thorough is by Michael Mott; see Mott, 561-68.

330. "Marxism and Monastic Perspectives," *Asian Journal*, 326-43.

331. The quotation is from the *Philokalia*, a collection of writings on the spiritual life, especially prayer of the heart, widely read in the Orthodox Church. A three-volume translation of the complete text is published by Faber & Faber.